THE LITTLE
RED BOOK
of
WINE LAW

A Case of Legal Issues

Cover design by ABA Publishing.

12 11 10 09 08   5 4 3 2 1

Library of Congress Cataloging-in-Publication Data

Carol Robertson
    The Little Red Book of Wine Law
    Carol Robertson
Library of Congress Cataloging-in-Publication Data is on file.

ISBN: 978-1-59031-988-8

Discounts are available for books ordered in bulk. Special consideration is given to state bars, CLE programs, and other bar-related organizations. Inquire at Book Publishing, ABA Publishing, American Bar Association, 321 North Clark Street, Chicago, Illinois 60654-7598.

www.ababooks.org

Dedication

This book is dedicated to my children,
Elisabeth Rochelle, Stephan, and Caelin,
all sharing their mother's enthusiasm
for good wine, good food, and exploring
the wine regions of California,
France, Germany, and Italy.

Table of Contents

Preface

When I was a young, impressionable college student, I received a scholarship from the Rotary Foundation to travel from Idaho, my home state, to Bordeaux, France, to study for a year. I tasted my first wines there and, understandably, thought all wines were of the same quality as a fine Bordeaux. It was, therefore, a surprise to return to do graduate work in California and realize that, on my student budget, the best wines I could afford were jugs of Gallo Hearty Burgundy® and Italian Swiss Colony California Chianti. However there were also many opportunities to drive up to Napa Valley and beyond into Mendocino County and the Russian River region to taste at the new wineries that seemed to open every day. And there were those special occasions that commanded a special wine: celebratory dinners with Puligny Montrachet, Château d'Yquem (yes, it was expensive but still affordable in those days), and toasts at weddings and graduation ceremonies with California sparkling wine or, when it was truly a grand event, a flute of Veuve Cliquot. Like many Americans at the time, I was initially untutored but learning to appreciate and value the wonderful world of wine, and eventually becoming passionate about all things connected with wine.

Americans have had a love/hate relationship with wine and other alcoholic beverages from colonial days. This passion is evidenced in the early laws and regulations, and in the cases interpreting the respective rights and responsibilities of those involved in the production and sale of wine in this country over the past century. This book loosely describes some of the milestones in wine history through the perspective of legal cases covering disputes among those involved in the wine industry from its early days at the turn of the nineteenth century through Prohibition and the rebuilding of this country after World War II to the increasing liberalization, deregulation, and globalization of the early twenty-first century.

One hundred years of wine making and sales are told through legal cases dating from 1910 to 2008. These 12 cases cover and interpret diverse subjects such as trademark law, antitrust law, criminal law, constitutional law, and even international treaties, but they all have one subject: wine production and sale. The emphasis of these cases is not entirely on California wineries; one case arises out of Washington state, another out of Illinois, and one each out of Michigan and New York state. However, it is not surprising that California wineries should be parties to more than one dispute, given that California today accounts for a large percentage of the wine production market in the United States, as it has for the past century. This has been a natural result of that state's climate and soils, its immigrant population, and also the vagaries of history, as we shall see. It is a fact that California-based wineries—E. & J. Gallo Winery, Kendall-Jackson Winery, and the Bronco Wine Company—happen to be the largest wine producers in the United States and have the substantial wealth necessary to endure lengthy litigation.

Interspersed through the book are short vignettes, summaries, or descriptions of topics mentioned in the cases, putting greater detail, for example, around trademark law as it pertains to wine, federal wine-labeling law, and state regulation of wine distribution. Some of the vignettes simply describe other legal disputes that provide a counterpoint to the cases, present a comparable dilemma, or simply tell a good wine-law story. And some provide useful information to those who desire a greater understanding of the wine industry and the legal framework for wine regulation.

The extensive migration of European immigrants to the United States in the latter part of the nineteenth century had a profound effect on the history of wine production. Some had been winemakers in their home countries of Germany, France, and Italy. And several eventually made their way to California to establish wineries. We count among these a German, whose winery, the Charles Krug Winery (the subject of Case 4 on labor issues), founded in 1861, was successful during its founder's lifetime, then fell into disrepair after his death but was rescued in 1943 by another famous immigrant family, this time Italian—Cesare Mondavi and his sons, Peter and Robert. A group of Italian immigrants joined with several Swiss to form the first successful large wine enterprise at the turn of the twentiethth century, Italian Swiss Colony (a brand that exists to this day), which is the subject of Case 1 involving a trademark dispute with yet another Italian-American-owned wine production company. Likewise, Case 3, an estate/family business ownership dispute, involves a family of three Italian immigrant brothers.

One of the most important events in the twentieth century for the alcoholic beverage industry was, of course, Prohibition. Case 2 involves a sting operation against a legally permitted winery (yes, they did exist, but only to produce "non-beverage" wine, which admittedly seems like an oxymoron) in New York City during the 1920s. And several cases, including the much-discussed U.S. Supreme Court decision in *Granholm v. Heald* (Case 9), involve the three-tier regulatory system for wine distribution that was put in place in many states when Prohibition was repealed in 1933, providing a window into the impacts of Prohibition and its permanent effect on the wine industry.

Case 4, involving labor troubles at the Charles Krug Winery, shows a different side of wine production and the history of California—the lives of the laborers who pick the grapes. In the 1970s, newspapers were filled with stories involving the legendary Cesar Chavez and the United Farm Workers (UFW) and their nationwide boycott of certain grape growers in California's Central Valley, including the E & J. Gallo Winery. The UFW's battle with the Charles Krug Winery was perhaps less discussed but was (and remains) longer-lasting and more illustrative of the ebb and flow of organized labor's influence. Rising union power in the 1970s led to the passage of the historic Agricultural Labor Relations Act in California in 1978; lessening influence has led to recent cancellations of union contracts in both Napa and Sonoma counties in the 2000s.

As the wine industry has grown in the last 30 years, change has been inevitable. The impact of this change is seen in three very different cases. First, the Napa Valley has become an international destination and is a far different place than it was in 1966, when Robert Mondavi established his historic winery along the St. Helena Highway. The impact of this growth on this bucolic valley is shown in Case 8, involving a road easement dispute. Second, the branding of wine is critical to the success of all wineries, and enormous sums are now paid to acquire, build, and protect a valued trademark. This impact is seen in Case 6, involving the brothers who founded the famous E. & J. Gallo Winery and their lawsuit to prevent the use of the Gallo trademark by their younger brother; in Case 7, involving a dispute between the E & J. Gallo Winery and Kendall-Jackson Winery over similar trade dress; and in Case 11, involving the use of the word "Napa" in wine labels. And third, related to the importance and value of a name, wine is now very much a global business, and the impact of this is seen in Case 12, where the United States was pitted against the European Union over the use of the EU's famous geographic names on wine (and beer) labels and the United States' protection of long-time trademarks that may have "borrowed" those place names.

A glass of champagne, anyone? Or would you prefer sparkling wine?

Introduction

A Brief History of
U.S. Wine (in America)—
A Methuselah[1] of Factoids
About Wine (and Law)

*From the early days of the founding of the colonies
that would become the United States, wine has been
a part of the history of America, and the fate of the
wine industry has been heavily influenced by the
cultural, political, and legal history of this country,
as well as its international relations.
To better appreciate some of the nuances
of the cases in this book, in a few pages,
200 years of wine history are summarized—
blended, if you wish—into assorted factoids
about wine, wine law, and the
people who make wine.*

---

1. A "Methuselah" is a bottle size, sometimes used in wine circles, from the French; a very large wine bottle comprising 6 liters or 8 standard Champagne bottles.

Year 1000

When he landed in North America in 1001, Leif Erikson was so impressed by its many grapevines that he named the newly discovered land "Vinland."

Year 1600

It is believed that among the first settlers to land in present-day Virginia and to found the Jamestown Colony was at least one winemaker. Some wine was likely produced using native vine hedge grapes, probably without much success, during the first year of the Colony's existence.[2]

One of the first local wines drunk by American colonists was made from the Scuppernong grape, a native grape.[3] *This grape is still made into wine in North Carolina.*[4]

The British hoped that its colonies in America would provide England with a new source for wine so that they would not have to continue to buy claret from the condescending French. In the early 1600s British Parliament enacted laws requiring that wine grapes be cultivated in the Virginia Colony and making the theft of grapes a capital crime.[5]

2. Gordon W. Murchie, *Virginia First in Wine*, GRAPEVINE MAGAZINE, Sept./Oct. 2005, *reprinted in* www.virginiawinefestival.org/downloads/Virginia%20First%20in%wine.pdf, at 1.

3. PAUL LUKACS, AMERICAN VINTAGE: THE RISE OF AMERICAN WINE 34 (Houghton Mifflin Co. 2000).

4. The Scuppernong grape produces a sweet dessert wine. The Scuppernong is the official state fruit of North Carolina. It is claimed to be the first grape actually cultivated in the United States. "Official State Symbols of North Carolina," *available at* http://statelibrary.dcr.nc.us/nc/symbols/symbols.htm.

5. Murchie, *supra* note 2 at 1.

Thomas Jefferson, while ambassador to France, took a great interest in wines from Bordeaux, and especially the wine from the Chateau d'Yquem. He planted vineyards at his estate in Monticello upon his return but was never able to produce a palatable bottle of wine from his own vineyard.[6]

President Washington favored wine from Europe, particularly Madeira wine from Portugal, which was the most popular imported wine in the new United States at that time.[7]

The native grapes used in early colonial wine production came to be known as "fox grapes," because of their decidedly "foxy" (musky) odor and flavor, which made the wine made from them undrinkable.[8]

European wines were produced from a species known as vitis vinifera; *American grapes were of a different species,* vitis labrusca. *American grapes grow in the wild; European grapes are cultivated and do poorly when not properly cared for.*

Attempts to grow European vinifera *grape varieties in the United States were not successful in the early nineteenth century due to extremes of climate in most parts of the eastern United States (freezing temperatures in the winter followed by hot and humid summers); the prevalence of downy mildew and black rot; and the dreaded phylloxera.*

---

6. LUKACS, *supra* note 3 at 15-17.
7. Murchie, *supra* note 2 at 2.
8. LUKACS, *supra* note 3 at 17; *see also* THOMAS PINNEY, A HISTORY OF WINE IN AMERICA: FROM THE BEGINNINGS TO PROHIBITION, Appx. 1, at 443-45 (Univ. of Cal. Pr. 1980), *available at* http://ark.cdlib.org.ark:/13030/ft967nb63q/.

In 1769, Franciscan missionary Father Junipero Serra planted the first California vineyard at Mission San Diego de Alcalá, using a vinifera *grape variety probably imported by Spanish settlers to Mexico, which became known as the "Mission" grape.*

The most successful wine from the California missions, using the Mission grape, was produced at Mission San Gabriel, a few miles east of what is now Los Angeles. Wine was also produced at the Sonoma Mission, the last and most northern of the chain of California missions. Because the Mission grape produced a flat-flavored, low-acid wine with high sugar content, it was fortified with brandy to maintain its residual sugar and named "angelica," after City of Angels.[9]

Year 1800

Winemaking in Los Angeles was first commercialized by a Frenchman appropriately named Jean Louis Vignes (French for "vines"), originally from Cadillac, in the Bordeaux region. In 1833, he imported and planted European varietals from France in California.[10] *However, the Mission grape continued to be the dominant variety in Los Angeles vineyards until after World War II.*

---

9. PINNEY, *id.* at 240-41.
10. LUKACS, *supra* note 3 at 61.

*A retired military man, Major John Adlum, using
certain American vines, developed native hybrids
in Maryland in the early 1800s and had particular
success with the Catawba grape, which grew well
in the Ohio Valley and in Missouri, two early wine-
producing areas.*[11]

*The Catawba grape was popularized by Nicholas
Longworth, a wealthy real estate investor in Cincinnati,
Ohio, before the Civil War, who used it in the production
of the first commercially successful sparkling wine.
The beverage sold well on the East Coast and was
memorialized by Longfellow in his "Ode to Catawba
Wine." The grape was a light purplish red color, yielding
a white wine somewhat reminiscent of white zinfandel,
but very dry. Catawba is featured today by some
wineries in the Ohio Valley.*

*Longworth was a believer in temperance who
experimented in grape cultivation and wine production
hoping that wine with a lower alcohol content would
replace whisky at American dinner tables.*[12]

*The Civil War introduced the Special Occupation Tax
(SOT), a tax on wine enacted to pay off war debt.*[13]
The tax was only repealed in 2005.[14]

---

11. *Id.* at 21-22.
12. LUKACS, *supra* note 3 at 14.
13. GAO, U.S. General Accounting Office Report to the Joint Committee on Taxation, U.S. Congress, Sept. 1990, *Alcohol Excise Taxes: Simplifying Rate Can Enhance Economic and Administrative Efficiency, available at* http://archive.gao.gov/f0102/142457.pdf. The excise tax remained in effect until 2005, when it was suspended for three years (from July 1, 2005, until June 30, 2008) by Act of Congress. The American Jobs Creation Act of 2004 (P.L. 108-357).
14. The Safe, Accountable, Flexible, Efficient Transportation Equity Act: A Legacy for Users (P.L. 109-59), effective July 1, 2008.

During the 1850s, Ohio was the undisputed national leader in grape production, representing approximately 35 percent of the national total, followed by California with 15 percent. By 1860, black rot and mildew had destroyed most Ohio vineyards.[15]

In 1851, Maine enacted the first statewide "prohibition" law, forbidding the manufacture and sale of alcoholic beverages within the state.[16]

Phylloxera, a tiny, aphid-like insect that attacks the roots of grapevines, was indigenous to the eastern United States but unknown outside North America until 1863, when some cuttings of American grapevines were taken to Europe. Phylloxera sucks nutrients from the roots of the vine, gradually starving it. By 1865, the insect had spread to vines in Provence, and over the next 20 years it nearly destroyed all European vineyards.[17]

The phylloxera blight in Europe resulted in shortages of wine for many years. This created an opportunity for California wines. Thirty-five medals were awarded to California wines at the Paris Exposition Universelle in 1889.[18]

---

15. Lake Erie Enology Research Center, Research: Introduction, *available at* http://www.us.ysu.edu/~enology/research.htm.

16. PINNEY, *supra* note 8 at 431.

17. LUKACS, *supra* note 3 at 36.

18. Paul Lukacs, *The Rise of American Wine,* AMERICANHERITAGE.COM, Dec. 1996, Vol. 47, Issue 8, *available at* http://www.americanheritage.com/articles/magazine/ah/1996/8/1996_8_84.shtml.

In the 1860s, several immigrants to Northern California imported large quantities of European varietals to replace the Mission grape. One of the most important of these was Colonel Agostan Haraszthy, a Hungarian soldier, who founded the Buena Vista Winery in Sonoma. (In 1946, the state of California dedicated a memorial to him as the "Father of California Viticulture." The plaque is located in the main plaza in the town of Sonoma in Northern California.)

Fraud and adulteration were growing problems in the 19th Century, and sloppy practices in the California wine industry prevented California from developing the reputation necessary to replace the French wineries as having the best wines.

Year 1880

In 1881, Andrea Sbarboro, a native of Genoa, launched a large grape-growing business as a cooperative experiment. It became known as The Italian Swiss Colony. Preference in the organization was given to Italians or Swiss who had become U.S. citizens or who had declared their intention of becoming citizens. By 1887, it had become a joint stock company and constructed a 300,000-gallon winery.[19]

By 1890, California produced most of the wine grown and made in the United States (60 percent).[20] New York was another important wine-producing state.

---

19. WILLIAM SEABROOK, AMERICANS ALL: A HUMAN STUDY OF AMERICAN CITIZENS FROM EUROPE 136 n.1 (George G. Harrap & Co., Ltd. 1938).
  20. PINNEY, *supra* note 8 at 315-17.

A native eastern United States grapevine resistant to phylloxera was used as root stock in grafting European varietal vines; by the mid-1890s, the European wine industry had begun to reestablish itself.

Year 1900

In 1915, California winemakers displayed their wares at the Panama-Pacific Exposition in San Francisco.

In 1915, the federal government increased the excise tax on brandy and other fortified wines from 3 cents a gallon to 55 cents.[21]

In 1919, the Volstead Act instituted National Prohibition in the United States, through the Eighteenth Amendment to the United States Constitution. The Amendment was repealed by the Twenty-first Amendment in 1933.

In December 1933, after Repeal, the E. & J. Gallo Winery made its first shipments of Gallo-branded wine.

In 1943, Cesare Mondavi purchased the defunct Charles Krug Winery in the Napa Valley, where his sons, Robert and Peter, began to produce quality varietal wines.

Year 1950

In the 1950s, the Charles Krug Winery was one of the first Napa Valley wineries to open a visitors' center where people could taste samples of Charles Krug-branded wines.

---

21. GAO Report to the Joint Committee on Taxation, U.S. Congress.

In 1965, Jack and Jamie Davies purchased the Schramsberg Estate and began producing quality sparkling wine, using the méthode champenoise, *the traditional method for making Champagne, developed in the Champagne region of northern France.*

In 1966, Robert Mondavi, following a dispute with his mother and brother over the management of the Charles Krug Winery, founded the Robert Mondavi Winery down the road in Oakville, California.

In 1973, Moët-Hennessy (Moët et Chandon) acquired land near Yountville and founded Domaine Chandon; its first California sparkling wine using the méthode champenoise *was released in 1976, and its visitors' center and famed restaurant opened in 1977.*

In 1976, at a blind tasting in Paris, the 1973 Stag's Leap Winery Cabernet Sauvignon took first place over the top Bordeaux red wines.

In 1977, the Gallo family began acquiring land in Sonoma County and began producing wines there in the early 1990s; Gallo of Sonoma was officially established in 1993, when its first wines were released.

In 1982, Jess Jackson, a San Francisco attorney, founded the Kendall-Jackson Winery, with a goal of producing quality wine at affordable prices.

Year 2000

In 2004, Constellation Brands, one of the largest wine producers in the United States, based in New York State, acquired the renowned Robert Mondavi Winery.

THE LITTLE
RED BOOK

of

WINE LAW

"Tipo Chianti": Can a Type of Red Be Trademarked?

Italian Swiss Colony v. Italian Vineyard Company,
158 Cal. 252 (1910)

I n 1938, William Seabrook, who was writing a book about the European immigrant experience in America, traveled to California.[1] The purpose of the trip was to interview members of first- and second-generation Italian-American families who had migrated to the United States at the turn of the twentieth century. One of his more interesting discoveries was the then-dominant positions that families of Italian origin had achieved in the production of California wine. By then, of course, Ernest and Julio Gallo were on their way to building their wine empire. Cesare Mondavi had settled in Lodi, where he was a well-known grape grower. Seabrook was particularly struck by the fact that most wine at the time was produced as either a generic red or white, with the red wine aged not in traditional oak but rather in huge redwood "vats, the gigantic bar-

---

1. SEABROOK, WILLIAM, AMERICANS ALL: A HUMAN STUDY OF AMERICAN CITIZENS FROM EUROPE (London: George G. Harrap & Co,, Ltd., 1938).

rels, which are sometimes as tall as a house," holding 50,000 or more gallons of wine.[2] *This wine was then shipped across the country in railroad tanks to be bottled in metropolitan cities such as Chicago and New York, where it was sold, usually under European-style place names, such as "California Burgundy" or "California Chablis."*

In the early 1970s, Italian Swiss Colony was a major brand of wine in the United States. Its television ads featured "the little old winemaker, me," a quaint old man in a Swiss national costume holding a glass of red wine, being kissed by a charming young Swiss maid. At that time, Americans were more likely to drink inexpensive jug wines than premium bottled wine. By then Italian Swiss Colony was an American institution. Its distinctive, straw-covered bottle graced many a college student's desk as a candle holder.

---

2. *Id.* at 137.

Italian Swiss Colony was a large winemaking cooperative that then dominated the California market. It was formed in 1881 when a group of Italian grape growers (with a few Swiss partners) collected $10,000 and bought vineyard land in the Sonoma Valley, north of San Francisco, that they named Asti. They gradually expanded their holdings along the north coastal region and into the Central Valley to the southeast and became one of the biggest wine producers in California, making approximately four million gallons per year by 1935.[3] In a large production warehouse that Italian Swiss Colony owned in San Francisco, it blended and bottled red and white wines from the various vineyards under its own label.[4]

Already in 1900, Italian Swiss Colony had gained market dominance as one of the largest sources of table wine in the United States[5] and had significant brand recognition. The company was particularly well known for producing a red wine that was commonly found in Italian homes and in family-style restaurants. This wine was sold in Italian Swiss Colony's now famous distinctive bottle—bulbous at the bottom, tapering to a narrow neck, and wrapped in a straw jacket similar to Italian Chianti bottles. It was called "Tipo Chianti." Over time, the wine gained popularity and was known to the public simply as "Tipo." According to Italian Swiss Colony's trademark application for Tipo, registered under the provisions of the federal Trademark Act of 1905 (which was the federal trademark statute in the United States at the time), the word "tipo" had never before been used by anyone in connection with the manufacture or sale of wine.

The Italian Vineyard Company was founded in 1900 by Sec-

---

3. *Id.* at 136, n.1.

4. *Biggest on the Vine*, TIME, Monday, April 27, 1953, http://www.time.com/magazine/article/0,9171,818339,00.html?promoid=googlep.

5. LUKACS, AMERICAN VINTAGE, p. 84.

When he landed in North America in 1001, Leif Erikson was so impressed by its many grapevines that he named the newly discovered land "Vinland."

ondo Guasti, an immigrant from the Piedmont region of Italy. By 1910, the company had become one of the largest wine producers in San Bernardino County, east of Los Angeles.[6] The Italian Vineyard Company labeled barrels and bottles of its red wine as "Tipo Barbera" and "Tipo Puglia." Its intent, the company claimed, was to let the consumer (who more than likely would have been a first-generation Italian immigrant buying dry wine for dinner) know that these red wines would have characteristics of the Barbera or Puglia regional wines of Italy. Italian Swiss Colony sued, alleging that the Italian Vineyard Company was using the word "Tipo," which was Italian Swiss Colony's exclusive trademark, in an effort to foist its wine on the unsuspecting public as the wine of Italian Swiss Colony and, thus, to benefit from Italian Swiss Colony's goodwill and reputation.

The court utilized two separate lines of analysis of the issues. The first related to the behavior of the defendant under common law—what was the Italian Vineyard Company's intent in using the word "Tipo" to identify its red wine? Did this constitute "unfair competition"? The second line questioned whether the Italian Vineyard Company had infringed on a trademark right of Italian Swiss Colony under the Trademark Act of 1905. In other words, was the use of the word "Tipo" on the Italian Vineyard Company's bottles of Barbera wine prohibited because of Italian Swiss Colony's registration of the word for use on wine?

---

6. *Id.* at 86.

If the Italian Vineyard Company were guilty of unfair competition in using the word "Tipo" on its wine labels, then the interpretation of the nature and extent of Italian Swiss Colony's trademark—or even whether it had a trademark—was not necessary. And Italian Swiss Colony pushed this argument: that in using the word "Tipo," which was so closely identified with Italian Swiss Colony's distinctive Chianti-style red wine, on its labels, the Italian Vineyard Company was attempting to deceive the public into believing that the defendant's red wine was the same as that sold under Italian Swiss Colony's label. The law, even at that time, was well settled that a person who seeks, by imitating a label or package, to induce consumers to buy from him in the belief that they are dealing with another, better-known producer has engaged in unfair competition. Although one dissenting judge thought Italian Swiss Colony had proved its argument, the majority could not find evidence of any intent to deceive on the part of the defendant. They noted that the Italian Vineyard Company had made no attempt to imitate Italian Swiss Colony's distinctive straw basket–encased bottle; its bottle was instead an "ordinary, straight-sided" (i.e., Bordeaux-style) claret bottle. The court also noted that the labels for the two wines were "totally different in size, shape, [and] color." The only point of resemblance was in the use of the word "Tipo."

Absent a claim of unfair competition, Italian Swiss Colony then had to demonstrate infringement under the 1905 Trademark Act. At that time, the requirement for proving infringement was to show that the defendant had made a colorable imitation of a trademark affixed to a product of substantially the same descriptive properties as those of the trademark owner. This was a very narrow test. If the Italian Vineyard Company had imitated Italian Swiss Colony's bottles and other trade dress, Italian Swiss Colony could have prevented the defendant from using that same mark on that type of bottle. But the law did not offer much more protection than that. Italian Swiss Colony could prevent the Italian Vineyard Company from using "Tipo" on its labels only if Italian Swiss Colony had the exclusive right to the word as a name for a wine. And it could claim such an exclusive right only if it owned "Tipo" as a valid trademark.

Therefore, the court considered whether the trademark "Tipo" that Italian Swiss Colony had registered under the 1905 Act was a distinctive mark, so that purchasers of wine sold under the "Tipo" label recognized that wine as being produced by Italian Swiss Colony. If that were the case, then under the 1905 Act, the Italian Vineyard Company would be prevented from applying the word "Tipo" to wine of the same description. The amount of protection afforded a claimed trademark depended upon how distinctive it was compared to the mark used by the trademark claimant's competitor—today, whether it would be classified as a so-called "strong mark." A strong mark generally is one that is so fanciful or unique that it has come to symbolize the maker of the product, while weak marks include those that are generic or describe the usual and the not so fanciful qualities of the product. The Trademark Act of 1905 was limited in the protection it offered, and marks that were not descriptive enough did not merit protection at all, no matter how closely they were identified with the product.

The court had to decide whether calling a wine "Tipo" involved employing a word in common usage, or whether Italian Swiss Colony's use of the word to identify its wine was unique and distinctive. In other words, did using the Italian word in an English-speaking market make it more like an invented term?

In Italian, the word, *tipo* means "type" or "kind." In the United States, if one were to use the English equivalent on a wine label, such as a "Bordeaux-type" wine, no one would consider it to be distinctive enough to merit trademark protection. It is too generic. So the majority in this case wondered, should Italian Swiss Colony be able to claim the exclusive right to use a term that basically means "Chianti-type wine"? In other words, should it have trademark protection for a word that in English would only be descriptive and nothing more? But the word used was not *type* but rather *tipo*, and, Italian Swiss Colony argued, that should make all the difference. This was particularly the case where, it claimed, its Chianti-style wine had become known to customers as "Tipo Red" and where they actually associated the word "Tipo" with wine produced by Italian Swiss Colony. The court, however, was not ready to accept this argument.

Instead it accepted the defendant's contrary argument that Italian Swiss Colony was only using "Tipo" in connection with its Chianti as a descriptive term to appeal to its typical customers— Italian-American immigrants, who in 1910 constituted the vast majority of dry red wine drinkers in the United States. These customers, upon seeing a bottle of Italian Swiss Colony red wine with a label describing it as "Tipo Chianti" on a shelf, would understand its Italian meaning perhaps even better than any English words and would equate it with a type of well-known Chianti wine produced in Italy. And, as the Italian Vineyard Company further argued, it was not imitating a Chianti-type wine but rather was producing red wines that had the characteristics of other Italian vintages, such as Barbera, and was simply marketing its wines to appeal to those same Italian-speaking consumers who might choose a wine of a type (*tipo*) that was reminiscent of their home country. In other words, there was no likelihood of confusion for consumers, because the wines produced by the two competing companies were not of the same descriptive quality.

Accordingly, the court ruled that Italian Swiss Colony did not have any trademark right to protect in the word "Tipo" on its

"Tipo Chianti" label and that the Italian Vineyard Company was free to sell its own Italian-type red wines as long as it did not do so in a way—such as by copying the packaging—that would lead the purchaser to believe that he was buying an Italian Swiss Colony wine.

At the time, the court elected not to address the issue of whether Italian Swiss Colony could claim a valid trademark right based upon the word "Tipo" standing alone. (By 1910, the wine was commonly referred to simply as "Tipo," but the label still tied the word "tipo" to "Chianti.") Today, the concept of dilution and the protection of a brand that had come to be associated with its original and more famous user are much more accepted, and Italian Swiss Colony may have been able to use this argument, but in 1910 these were still unfamiliar concepts, and the court did not pursue that avenue.

The question of when a wine label should receive special protection has not gone away, as we will see in Case 7—a recent case involving the use of grapevines on a wine label. There are only so many ways to identify a wine and still inform the buyer of the nature and quality of the product in the bottle. Of course, Italian Swiss Colony ultimately won out in the competitive war, growing to become for a time one of the largest producers of bulk wines in the United States, while the Italian Vineyard Company is now only a name from an earlier period in California's wine history.[7]

---

7. Italian Swiss Colony is best known today as a souvenir of the past, as much as the "little old winemaker" from its ads, and as one of the many brands now owned by Constellation Brands, which in 2004 also acquired The Robert Mondavi Corp. in an acrimonious takeover opposed by the Mondavi family. *See* Julia Flynn Siler, The House of Mondavi: The Rise and Fall of an American Wine Dynasty 356-57 (Gotham Books 2007).

Vignette

California Wine in 1908

"As I was tasting the so-called ports, sherries, tokays, Angelicas, burgundies or sauternes, I made a comment about the 'sherry' which would have been equally apropos to them all. I said, 'Look, this is a good wine, fine body, fine flavour— but it doesn't taste anything like sherry.'"[1]

If you were to travel to a California winery in the 1870s, or for that matter before the 1970s, you would have thought yourself in a different place from today's California wine milieu. It was definitely a different time. Few people drank quality wine, and those who did generally imported theirs from France. California wine was known to many as an inferior drink favored by poor immigrants and winos. As a general rule, the wines were blended from different varieties of grapes from a range of vineyards, and to combat the astringency of the wine and to add an alcohol "kick," brandy was not infrequently added to increase the alcohol content. Many wines were made from the common Mission grape, one of the first of the European varietals to thrive in California, brought there originally in the 1700s by the Franciscan friars as they established their chain of missions from San Diego in the south to as far north as Sonoma County. The Mission grape thrived in the dry, sunny climate of Los Angeles and San Bernardino County, and The Old Mission Winery, owned by Antonio Moramarco,[2] produced a typical wine of the era, which is described in the quotation that introduced this vignette. It was a sweet wine, frequently fortified to produce a California Port or a California Brandy.

A correspondent for *The New York Times*, on a visit to San Francisco in 1876 to celebrate the United States Centennial, commented, on tasting some wines produced at the time in California's Central Valley, that these were

"atrocious—absolutely unequaled in villainy by the worst efforts that have been made in the same direction in New

11

Vignette (continued)

Jersey or Nebraska. In both of these States I have tasted wine that was excruciating, that left a memory upon the palate like a great sorrow. But . . . . I have never been swindled into swallowing anything half as vile as some claret made by a Frenchman in the old mission of San Jose. . . ."[3]

The problem for California wines then, which would continue for almost a century, was that good wines were being made even as early as the 1870s in California, but the market was dominated by large bulk wine producers, such as Italian Swiss Colony and later the Gallo brothers, who favored a blended wine that was consistent, an average wine, better than many *"vins ordinaires"* produced at the time in France as an everyday table wine, but also a wine that was not intended to nor destined to be great. This was a wine that sought to appeal to the palates of Americans, who favored drinks with a high alcohol content, such as whiskey and, later, gin and vodka. When Americans selected an alcoholic beverage, they sought not subtlety but strong flavor, with a kick.[4] Many wines from the time, particularly those made with the easy-to-grow and easy-to-ship Mission grape, were fortified to give Americans what they wanted.

In another article in *The New York Times* from June 1874, the correspondent in San Francisco noted:

"There is an increasing demand in our Eastern cities for California wine, but it is not a healthy or encouraging demand. The wine is used a great deal in making other wines, or sold in poor restaurants. One seldom sees a California wine on gentlemen's tables. It has not a good name. It is considered heady and liable to be 'doctored.'"[5]

At the time that this correspondent visited Northern California, there were actually some good California wines even though, as a general rule, they were not exported, perhaps because they did not have a high enough alcohol content to survive the rough treatment in travel. Those that were sent

abroad were well regarded and
frequently won prizes. But the
general reputation of the wines
as something of poor quality and
adulterated was reinforced by East
Coast critics, who tended to view
the wines as second-rate to the
European wines that they were
more likely to consume. Good
wine makers could be found in
Northern California particularly—
for example, Charles Krug—but
what was needed was for the
larger of these wineries to use
better quality control not only
in the production of their wines
but also in their distribution
to ensure that when they were
exported to other parts of the
country, through trustworthy and

respected agents, they arrived in a condition to be appreciated.
Until that happened, the *Times* correspondent foretold, California
wines would continue to be distrusted and subject to criticism.[6]

These early critiques of California wine production could
just as easily have been published a century later, in the early
1970s: most California wine in 1870 (and in 1970) was blended,
at best bland, and at worst too doctored to be good. Too much
mediocre wine was converted into brandy or other fortified wine,
such as a port or a sherry. But it was also the case in 1870 (and
in 1970) that there were some winemakers who were honest in
their craft, experimenting with varieties of grapes other than
the Mission grape, and who were successful in producing
good, subtle, prize-winning wines—as good as any at the time
in France or Italy. The writer of the 1877 *New York Times* article
who had encountered the "vile" wine in San Jose located another
vintner nearby who served him a glass of Zinfandel that he

Vignette (continued)

described as a "generous, full-bodied red wine." During that same visit to Northern California in December 1876, he also tasted some of the sparkling wines that had been bottled a few years before by Agoston Haraszthy, the founder of Buena Vista Winery. (It is thought that the Buena Vista Winery under Haraszthy produced the first sparkling wine in California, called Eclipse.)[7]

The wine was "faultless," the writer said, "good in flavor, exceedingly full-bodied, very sparkling, very dry. . ." Over a century ago, adjectives were used to describe the flavor of a contemporary wine that could be used to describe a fine California sparkling wine today. But something caused time to stop in the near century between the publication of this article in *The New York Times* in 1876 and the beginning of the new Renaissance in California wines that began in the early 1970s and continued through the last three decades of the twentieth century. That "something" was national Prohibition.

---

1. SEABROOK, AMERICANS ALL 135.

2. The subject of Case 3: "Breaking Up Is Hard to Do: Wine as a Family Business."

3. *California's Vintage: The Golden Wine of the Pacific Coast*, N.Y. TIMES, Jan. 7, 1877 [available at *The New York Times* Archive] http://query.nytimes.com/gst/abstract.html/2res=9B04ESD6133AE63BBC4F53DFB766838C669FDE.

4. Ironically, this is a critique that has been leveled at Robert Parker, the influential wine critic, justly or unjustly—that he favors big, bold wines, such as robust Zinfandels and heady Cabernet Sauvignons, with a higher alcohol level than has traditionally been the case for red wine, so-called "fruit bombs."

5. *Winemaking in California*, N.Y. TIMES, June 29, 1874 [available at *The New York Times* Archive].

6. *Id.*

7. Released in 1860. Heidi Cusick-Dickerson, Richard Gillette, Rodney Strong, "Buena Vista Winery," SONOMA: THE ULTIMATE WINERY GUIDE, Revised and Updated, 2nd Ed., Chronicle Books 2005, 36-37.Unfortunately, Haraszthy did not live long enough to see the success of his wines. He was lost and is presumed to have died, perhaps eaten by an alligator in the Brazilian jungle, where he traveled after leaving the California wine business.

When Is Wine Not a Beverage?

Dumbra v. United States, 268 U.S. 435 (1925)

T he Catawba grape was popularized by Nicholas Longworth, a wealthy real estate investor in Cincinnati, Ohio,
before the Civil War, who used it in the production of the
*first commercially successful sparkling wine. The beverage
sold well onthe East Coast and was memorialized by Longfellow in his "Ode to Catawba Wine." The grape was a light purplish red color, yielding a white wine somewhat reminiscent of
white zinfandel, but very dry. Catawba is featured today by
some wineries in the Ohio Valley.*

*Longworth was a believer in temperance who experiment-
ed in grape cultivation and wine production hoping that wine
with a lower alcohol content would replace whisky at American
dinner tables.*[1]

When the Volstead Act—the Eighteenth Amendment to the United States Constitution—was ratified and became effective on
January 1, 1920, the United States entered into a "dark age" of
wine history. This Amendment—which brought in national Pro-

---

1. LUKACS, *supra* note 3 at 14.

hibition—temporarily halted the development of the U.S. wine industry and completely changed the business of the production and sale of wine in this country. Prohibition was not a sudden event. For many years before 1919 there had been a groundswell across the country against "demon alcohol," and wine (and wine making) was in a sense a victim in the battle against a much greater evil: high-alcohol-content beverages such as whiskey.

It is important to understand that throughout the nineteenth century, most Americans were not wine drinkers, but many drank other alcoholic beverages heavily. When Thomas Jefferson attempted to import European vines into Virginia to create an American-based wine agriculture, and when Nicholas Longworth spent millions of dollars establishing a short-lived wine industry in Ohio,[2] these men did not do so merely because they appreciated fine wines (although Jefferson in particular had developed a taste for good Bordeaux vintages during his years as ambassador to France), but largely because they saw wine as something more natural, purer, and with a much lower alcohol content than the whiskey and rum that were the daily beverages of many Americans at the time.[3] What else could they drink? They had no access to fruit juices (which would have spoiled quickly with no refrigeration), their water was disease-ridden, and milk also would have spoiled quickly. By all accounts, Americans in the nineteenth century spent their days in a semi-drunken stupor, and the Eighteenth Amendment was seen as a means to bring America back to sobriety.

Although the prohibition of the Eighteenth Amendment seems absolute, there were several loopholes in the law. For ex-

---

2. Nicholas Longworth was an early promoter of wine as an aid to temperance. *See,* Timothy O. Rice, *Nicholas Longworth: Father of the American Wine Industry,* WINERY INSIGHT, July 2003, http://www.weekendwinery.com/wineryinsight/Article.Jul 03.htm.

3. PINNEY, A HISTORY OF WINE IN AMERICA 435.

ample, each home was allowed to make 200 gallons of "non-intoxicating cider and fruit juice" per year.[4] (Growers in California shipped grapes and so-called "grape juice bricks" throughout the United States to home producers, who made their own wine by adding yeast and allowing their "juice" to ferment.) Another loophole allowed the production of sacramental and medicinal wines under license from the federal government.[5] This was the loophole under which the Dumbras operated their winery in 1925.

The *Dumbra* case involved a classic sting operation. The Dumbras operated two separate businesses out of adjoining buildings on East 16th Street in New York City in the 1920s. In one, No. 514, they maintained a grocery store from which they sold dry goods, fruits, and vegetables. Next door, at No. 512, they operated a winery for the production of sacramental wine, under a permit from the government. This permit allowed them to manufacture and sell wines for non-alcoholic beverage purposes, and to keep on hand no more than 100,000 gallons of wine.

Under a search warrant, federal agents raided both of the Dumbras's businesses and hauled off 74 bottles of wine from the grocery store at No. 514 and 50 barrels of wine from the winery at No. 512. The Dumbras claimed that this was an unreasonable search and seizure without probable cause and, therefore, in violation of the Fourth Amendment to the U.S. Constitution. They asked the court to overturn the warrant as to the 50 barrels of wine. They argued that the warrant had been issued under false evidence given by an undercover federal agent. They also claimed that it had been issued in error because they held a permit to legally produce and sell the wine. This case made its way to the United States Supreme Court.

4. Volstead Act, 27 U.S.C. §46.
5. *Id.*

Acting on an anonymous tip that anyone could buy wine for the asking at the Dumbras's grocery store, undercover agents pretended to be customers. Once, an agent went into the grocery store and asked Mrs. Dumbra for two gallons of wine. She sent her son to the back of the store. The agent claimed in his affidavit that he saw Mrs. Dumbra's son turn right, in the direction of the winery, and soon he returned with the two gallons of wine. The Dumbras claimed there was no evidence that the wine had come from the winery. (The Dumbras did not challenge the seizure of the bottles of wine from the store.) However, on another occasion, the agent again visited the store and asked for one gallon of wine. This time, Mrs. Dumbra's son told the agent to wait outside. Soon after, the son came out the winery door and sold the wine to the agent in the street, outside the winery, and not in the grocery store. The son did not ask the agent to provide any documents showing that he was authorized to buy the wine for religious purposes.[6]

The Court considered the legitimacy of the affidavit on which the warrant was based. Because the Dumbras had a permit to make and sell wine legally for *non-beverage* purposes, the Court wondered if this allowed them to avoid a search and seizure. The agent had failed to tell the judge who issued the warrant for the search that the Dumbras had this permit. This failure did not please Justice Stone, who delivered the majority opinion in the case. However, he also noted that the Dumbras's permit did not authorize them to possess or sell intoxicating liquors for *beverage* purposes. If that was their intent, then the fact that they had a permit to sell wine for non-beverage purposes was irrelevant.

---

6. Under Section 6 of the Volstead Act, the seller had to retain a copy of the buyer's authorization to purchase.

And in the end, the Dumbras's very well-known readiness to sell wine to casual purchasers without inquiry as to the right of the buyer to purchase sacramental wine proved to be their downfall. The fact that an actual sale from the winery premises had taken place under suspicious circumstances would have been sufficient grounds for the judge to issue the warrant, according to the Court, even if he had known about the existence of the permit. It was true, the Court conceded, that the federal agent should have been more forthcoming with the judge, but the Dumbras's actual unlawful sales overrode any niceties as to how the warrant was issued. The sale to the agent in itself was sufficient to show probable cause, and the warrant was therefore allowed to stand. The Dumbras did not get back their 50 gallons of wine and likely suffered other consequences as well.[7]

As this case demonstrates, there were both short- and long-term consequences of Prohibition. One of the most serious short-term effects was the growing willingness of otherwise law-abiding citizens, such as the Dumbra family, to casually engage in illegal acts. It is likely that large quantities of so-called sacramental wines made for non-beverage purposes were ultimately consumed as beverages in places other than churches. Little boys were sent to drugstores to buy medicinal champagne and brandy for their aunts and grandmothers. People bought concentrated "grape juice" bricks and "wine loaves" that carried warnings on their labels to not add water or the ingredients were likely to ferment into wine.[8]

The father of Robert Mondavi first saw California when he went there on behalf of his fellow Italian compatriots back in

---

7. The penalties under the Volstead Act were small fines and, at worst, six months imprisonment, until 1929, when penalties were stiffened substantially under the Jones Act.

8. Called "Vine-Glo," *see* PINNEY, A HISTORY OF WINE IN AMERICA, 28-30.

Minnesota to buy grapes for them to make their 200-gallon annual allotment of home-fermented fruit juice.[9] And there is little doubt that organized crime gained entry into the liquor business because legitimate sources were outlawed under Prohibition. As more and more people came to disregard the law, public opinion turned against it. Nevertheless, not everyone was pleased when, in 1933, through the Twenty-first Amendment to the U.S. Constitution, the Eighteenth Amendment was repealed and the federal experiment in Prohibition ended.

Long-term consequences remain. It is likely that the fine-wine industry in the United States would have continued to develop, and with robust wineries in more states, if the American view of wine had not solidified during Prohibition as something dangerous, exciting, and illicit. In addition, Prohibition and its repeal led to a myriad of local and state laws regulating the manufacture, distribution, and sale of alcoholic beverages, which have had a long-lasting impact on wine consumption, the cost of wine in many parts of the country, the choices of wines available for purchase in different states, and, some would argue, the imposing market share that the California wine industry enjoys over other wine-producing regions in the United States.

---

9. SILER, THE HOUSE OF MONDAVI 12.

Vignette

National Prohibition and Its Aftermath

On January 1, 1920, national Prohibition became effective through the Eighteenth Amendment to the U.S. Constitution. Section 1 of the Amendment provided:

> [T]he manufacture, sale, or transportation of intoxicating liquors within, the importation thereof into, or the exportation thereof from the United States and all territory subject to the jurisdiction thereof for beverage purposes is hereby prohibited.

Prohibition remained in effect until the Amendment was repealed in December 1933. Despite its purpose of combating alcoholism (and the consumption of alcoholic beverages) in the United States, the law had a contrary effect. In fact, during this period wine consumption in the United States continued and may have actually increased.[1]

This did not mean that Prohibition had a minimal effect on the wine industry. Many wineries did not survive Prohibition. And the interruption in the development of wine production had nefarious effects that continue to be felt and that are reflected in recent legal battles among large and small wine producers, distributors, and state government regulators.

Prohibition didn't just happen. Although the dislocations and changes in the country during World War I may have had some effect, the success of the temperance movement was the result of a progressive movement that grew in strength during the nineteenth century. It also was not, as many believed, the natural impact of Puritanism on American life. The Puritans in fact were not abstainers: the first arrivals in Massachusetts Bay planted vineyards for wine.[2] Total abstinence was not in question. But temperance was the ideal. Both Thomas Jefferson and Nicholas Longworth promoted wine and wine production; they were part of a growing number of influential people in the early nineteenth century who saw increased wine consumption as an antidote to the stronger alcoholic beverages—rum and whiskey—that were staples in many American homes. Whiskey was cheap and available; water quality was poor. And these beverages were largely untaxed. Americans drank heavily almost daily, and there was strong evidence of the destructive effect of heavy spirit drinking.[3]

What had started as a relatively disorganized temperance movement gained momentum by the end of the nineteenth century. Cities enacted the first "dry" laws even before the Civil War. In 1851, Maine was the first state to pass a law prohibiting all intoxicating liquors.[4] Other states followed within the next few years. Even in California, dry communities were formed, such as Compton and Long Beach, right in the heart of the Los Angeles wine industry.[5] By 1917, momentum had grown sufficiently to enable the enactment of a national prohibition act. It was easily ratified as a constitutional amendment.

Once national Prohibition was achieved, however, only rudimentary enforcement took place. Policing the law was left not to the Justice Department but rather to the Internal Revenue Service. The Commissioner was empowered to appoint regional inspectors who had search and seizure powers, and courts levied fines. But generally, enforcement was lax. It seemed that proponents naively believed that once the law was passed, it would be obeyed. This was not the case. Once the law was enacted, it seemed that a large majority of Americans set about breaking it.

Prohibition had a disastrous effect on most wineries within the United States. Many wine producers had thought themselves to be different from distillers and breweries and took a wait-and-see approach to the prohibition movement until it was too late to develop a cohesive opposition. Believing that wine was a drink of temperance, not intoxication, many hoped that an exception would be created in the law for wine production. This did not happen. But because of these assumptions, winemakers were caught in the middle of the battle, unwilling to ally themselves

with the "demon" rum distillers and not wanting to join the cause of the prohibitionists in campaigning for the law (with an exception for their industry). As a result of Prohibition, regular wine trade was shut down, but what grew out of Prohibition were "back door" means of obtaining wine.

Exceptions to the Volstead Act allowed the production of sacramental wine under permit, and a few wineries were able to continue in operation on a limited basis under this guise. Wine could also be produced for other non-beverage purposes, such as for medicine or vinegar production. Section 29 of the Act allowed individuals to make non-alcoholic wine—in effect, grape juice.[6] Some enterprising winemakers produced juice concentrate and so-called "wine bricks" that were sold with

Vignette (continued)

yeast and a warning against illegal fermentation. Ironically, this allowance led to a large increase in vineyard planting, as a demand for fresh grapes for juice production opened up. Ultimately, the increased supply of vineyards led to negative consequences for the future wine industry, as wineries converted from high-quality wine grapes to varieties, such as Alicante Bouschet, which could survive shipment to home winemakers in other parts of the country. Alicante Bouschet is an intensely colored but essentially flat-flavored grape that was cultivated mainly to add color to wines. By itself, however, it made a decidedly mediocre wine, loaded with color and very little flavor.

The Twenty-first Amendment to the Constitution was ratified and became effective on December 5, 1933. Section 1 states simply: "The eighteenth article of amendment to the Constitution of the United States is hereby repealed." In *United States v. Chambers*,[7] the Supreme Court held that the National Prohibition Act, insofar as it relied on the Eighteenth Amendment, had become inoperative, with the result that prosecutions for violations of the Act, including proceedings on appeal, had to be dismissed.

By the time Prohibition ended in 1933, there were far too many grapes on the market, and the bottom fell out in prices. Furthermore, the push to plant vineyards with grapes such as Alicante Bouschet or the Thompson seedless grape meant that once Prohibition ended, grapes available for wine production in California were of poor quality, leading to an influx of ordinary blended wines that further damaged the reputation of California wines. The entire industry had to be rebuilt over the next decades.

---

1. Pinney, A History of Wine in America 436.
2. *Id.* at 29-30, 426.
3. *Id.* at 427.
4. *Id.* at 431.
5. *Id.* at 432-33.
6. "Allowed" meant that penalties were not imposed on home production, Volstead Act, 27 U.S.C. §46.
7. 291 U.S. 217, 222-26 (1934).

Breaking Up Is Hard to Do:
Wine as a Family Business

The Estate of Antonio Moramarco v. J. Moramarco,
86 Cal. App. 2d 326 (2d Dist. 1948)

He is a Spartan bachelor who does not go in for luxuries or frivolities. His office is crude, simple, carpetless as it was forty years ago, and he makes his rich, elegant *[emphasis added]* young nephews and nieces work in the wineries so they will know what they are inheriting when he dies.[1]

Two brothers, grown men, argue to the point of a fistfight in their mother's front yard. After the murder-suicide of their parents, two brothers go on to develop one of the largest wineries in the world, but fail to include their little brother in the venture.

A younger brother allows his older sibling, the true owner of the family wine chateau, to live in a two-bedroom apartment in Paris while he lives the luxurious life as a Count in Bordeaux.

---

1. SEABROOK, AMERICANS ALL, p. 135, describing his meeting with Antonio Moramarco.

29

A son sues his dying mother, accusing her of cheating him out of his shares in the family business.

Dysfunctional families can be found in any business, but the wine business seems to have more than its share. Although family wineries' glowing histories on their Web sites often describe the family's simple immigrant roots—ordinary people engaged in a family agricultural business—there is something not so simple about wine. Wine is romantic, passionate. Winemakers function as an aristocracy, whether in France or Italy or in the democratic United States.[2] And it seems nothing stirs the passions more than the battle for control in one of these businesses. It is particularly the hand-down of the business from the patriarch to the second generation that is hard. Usually these men are strong personalities who dominate the business and retain control much longer than they should. This creates significant transition issues.

In 1965, Robert Mondavi, then general manager of the Charles Krug Winery, had an argument with his younger brother, Peter, which led to the famously documented fistfight. As a result, Robert's mother, Rosa, threw Robert out of the business founded by Robert's father, Cesare Mondavi, forcing him in his fifties to strike out on his own and to found what became the world-famous Robert Mondavi Winery. He sued his mother and brother and ultimately obtained a multimillion-dollar settlement.[3]

In 1986, Ernest and Julio Gallo sued their younger brother,

---

2. In her history of the Robert Mondavi family, whose parents had been simple Italian peasants, Julia Flynn Siler describes the pleasure that Robert Mondavi and his son, Michael, derived from being invited to be members of the Primum Familiae Vini (First Families of Wine) as the sole American members—a society that included noble Italian and French families (namely, the Antinoris and the Rothschilds) who considered themselves an exclusive wine aristocracy. THE HOUSE OF MONDAVI, p. 228.

3. Siler, HOUSE OF MONDAVI, 123-124.

Joseph, for trademark infringement in a case described by the court as "sibling rivalry" of untold bitterness.[4]

In Bordeaux, a dispute among some 40 heirs to the famous Château d'Yquem led to the breakup and sale of a winery that had been in the same family since before the French revolution to a large corporate conglomerate.[5]

John Davies, son of Jack and Jamie Davies, the founders of the Schramsberg Estate (makers of the renowned California sparkling wine), sued his mother in California Superior Court, claiming that she had cheated him out of his interest in the winery business. Jamie Davies died before the legal dispute could settle.[6]

There is a reason that *Falcon Crest*, a television soap opera in the 1980s, had such a large following. These disputes make a good story, particularly when they involve the division of properties upon the death of the patriarch. It seems that, with wine estates in particular, there is a reluctance to give up control, to pass along the responsibility to the younger generation; there is the sense that only the father (or mother) is able to run the business as it ought to be run.[7] And sometimes it is simply because the patriarch does not expect to die.

This reluctance was evident in the case of Antonio Moramarco, patriarch of an Italian-American wine-making family in the early part of the twentieth century. He died of natural causes—

---

4. *See* Case 6: "Blood Is Not Thicker than Wine—The Gallo Family Feud."

5. *See* Vignette: "A Noble Battle—The Fight for Control of the Chateau d'Yquem."

6. Stacy Finz, *Jamie Davies Dies—Schramsberg Owner*, THE SAN FRANCISCO CHRONICLE, Thurs., Feb. 14, 2008, http://www.sfgate.com/cgi-bin/article.cgi?f=/c/a/2008/02/14/BAFQVIPMG.DTL&hw=Schramsberg&sn=002&sc=691.

7. Witness Robert Mondavi, who, after having had such a bitter dispute with his own brother for control of the family winery, engaged in behavior comparable to that of his father, retaining actual control of the Robert Mondavi Winery long after his two sons had taken on positions of apparent authority in the business. SILER, THE HOUSE OF MONDAVI.

The most successful wine from the California missions, using the Mission grape, was produced at Mission San Gabriel, a few miles east of what is now Los Angeles. Wine was also produced at the Sonoma Mission, the last and most northern of the chain of California missions. Because the Mission grape produced a flat-flavored, low-acid wine with high sugar content, it was fortified with brandy to maintain its residual sugar and named "angelica," after City of Angels.[8]

unfortunately, without leaving his will in a safe place. The Moramarco family, by all descriptions, seemed more unified than some other Italian-American wine-making families (such as the Mondavis), but there was sufficient dissension to spark a lawsuit after Antonio's death that went as far as the California appellate courts for resolution of the question of which family members would be entitled to share in the significant estate that Antonio had left behind.

The facts disclosed in *The Estate of Antonio Moramarco* leave much to the imagination over the causes of the dispute. Details of the Moramarco brothers' life are available through a family history posted on the Internet,[9] and these give the reader an insight into the nature of the relationship among Antonio and his other brothers, and the second generation's expectations. One must read between the lines and guess at some facts, but the story is that of a poverty-stricken Italian family that sent three of its four sons to seek a better fortune across the Atlantic at the

---

8. PINNEY, *id.* at 240-41.
9. *Our Moramarco Family History,* http://www.moramarco.net.

turn of the twentieth century. In the corners of this case lurks an untold story—that of the one son who stayed behind with his parents, and the suffering of his children in Mussolini's war-torn Italy.

There were four Moramarco brothers, born into a poor farming family in eastern Italy, inland from the Adriatic Sea, in the Altamura region. Antonio Moramarco, the eldest son, came to the United States in 1905. Once settled and employed, he sent for his brothers to help him establish his business in America. His brother Giuseppe (Joe) came over in 1906, and their brother Nicola (Nick) arrived shortly after. The three brothers migrated to Southern California and worked to establish a new business. They became United States citizens. They lived together at first, all in a small house where Antonio Moramarco's winery was located. Joe and Nick married and had children who worked in the family business when they were old enough. Antonio never married.

The fourth Moramarco brother, Francesco (Frank), did not join his brothers in California, but rather stayed behind in Italy. The court noted that he never came to the United States to see his brothers. (Is that fact so surprising in an era when steamship passage, even in steerage, would have been prohibitively expensive for a poor Italian man?) Frank never sent any money to invest in the winery. (Again, this is not surprising, given the impoverished conditions in which the Italian side of the family had lived in the early part of the twentieth century. It is unlikely that Frank Moramarco would have been in a position to make such an investment. But this fact was important to the outcome of the case.)

Over time, the brothers built a profitable fruit wholesale business. They bought a ranch property in Van Nuys and planted fruit trees, and other land where they grew cash crops, including grapes, and they owned a small winery, the Moramarco Brothers

Winemaking in Los Angeles was first commercialized by a Frenchman appropriately named Jean Louis Vignes (French for "vines"), originally from Cadillac, in the Bordeaux region. In 1833, he imported and planted European varietals from France in California. However, the Mission grape continued to be the dominant variety in Los Angeles vineyards until after World War II.

Winery. The farming and winery operations were a family affair, but without much formal accounting. In its description of the facts, the Court was careful to point out that all three brothers devoted their time to the winery and agricultural business and invested their money in it. For the most part, none of the Moramarco children received salaries for their work in the family business. It was just expected that they would help out. The three brothers combined their efforts and reinvested their earnings. Business was conducted as if a partnership existed among the brothers, but Antonio Moramarco, as the elder brother, was the acknowledged head of the family enterprise—the patriarch—and no written partnership agreement was created. For the most part, all the family assets were held in his name.

In the 1920s, during Prohibition, the brothers purchased the Old Mission Winery for what they considered "a good price."[10] It seems surprising that anyone would have thought it a sound

10. *Id.*

business idea to buy a winery in the middle of Prohibition. It was certainly a contrarian decision. Many winery businesses in California and elsewhere were forced to shut their doors after the Eighteenth Amendment was ratified. But, as in most things that Antonio Moramarco invested in, the winery purchase seems to have worked out very well. The Old Mission Winery produced sacramental wines and wines for medicinal purposes, both of which were legal under Prohibition. And the winery thrived once Prohibition was repealed in 1933. Antonio Moramarco proved himself to be an astute businessman.[11]

The three Moramarco brothers in Los Angeles lost contact with their brother who had stayed behind in Italy. As the court noted, Frank Moramarco never came to see Antonio or the other family members in California. Antonio visited Italy in 1922, but after that visit, he heard nothing more from Frank or his family, nor did he communicate further with them. Frank died sometime after that visit, and none of his children wrote to Antonio to let him know. This fact was important to the court's decision.

Antonio had made a will that was witnessed by his business manager, a Mr. Pollack, and Mr. Pollack's wife, Olga. Mr. Pollack testified at the trial that Antonio had intended to leave everything to his two brothers and did not want to leave anything to his brother Frank, who at the time was still alive in Italy, "Because," he allegedly said, "Mussolini is going to take it away from him." Mr. Pollack also testified that when Antonio's brother Nick died, Antonio expressed concern that Nick's children might not inherit Nick's half of Antonio's property at his own death and wondered if he should rewrite his will. But apparently he did nothing further, and there was no further acknowledgment of the existence of the Moramarco family members in Italy.

---

11. Seabrook, Americans All, pp. 135-36.

In November 1944, as Antonio was heading back to Los Angeles from a visit to the family vineyards, he suffered a fatal heart attack. Unfortunately, after his death, his will could not be found. However, when sorting through some business papers that had been shoved into a box when Antonio had moved his offices at some point, Mr. Pollack discovered a carbon copy of the will that he had witnessed years before. Although it was unusual, the court allowed the Moramarco estate to be probated on the basis of this copy, and the assets of Antonio Moramarco were distributed to his surviving California family members in accordance with its provisions. Because the will did not account for Antonio's nieces and nephews who were living in Italy (Frank's children), they received nothing. Somehow, despite the great distance between Italy and California and the silence between the two branches of the family for more than a decade, and during a World War in which the two countries had been on opposite sides, Frank's children learned of the will, and they sued to have the copy put aside. They argued that allowing the probate of a carbon copy of a will (where an alleged original had gone missing) was not in accordance with California Probate Law.[12] The result was a bitter battle that went to the California appellate courts. Frank's children had an incentive to put aside the will because, if it were shown that Antonio Moramarco had died intestate, as his heirs, they would have inherited one-third of his substantial estate.

One can imagine these survivors of a terrible World War arriving in California to claim a better life from their wealthier Cal-

---

12. Then, California Probate Code § 350 read as follows: "[no] will shall be proven as a lost or destroyed will unless proved to have been in existence at the time of . . . death . . . , or shown to have been destroyed fraudulently or by public calamity in the lifetime of the [deceased] . . .unless its provisions are clearly or distinctly proved by at least two credible witnesses."

ifornia cousins. One imagines also, however, the anger that Antonio's sole surviving brother felt at these children who had not deigned during Antonio's life to write or to contribute to the family enterprise and who only appeared after Antonio's death to claim a share of all they (he and his children and Nick's children) had worked for during Antonio's life. Where were these cousins when Joe and his children were spending their weekends and summers working in Uncle Tony's fields and wine cellars?[13] And it must be questioned whether they, even though Italian-Americans, possibly felt a small part of anti-Italian bias against their cousins, so soon after World War II. The Moramarcos had pointed out in their family history that the entire family had worked in the war effort and that several of Antonio's nephews had fought in Europe during the War.[14] Such a bias against Mussolini and Italy, the country that had been an enemy of the United States, is an undercurrent in this case, decided so soon after the end of the war. In any event, the court demonstrated little sympathy toward these newfound Italian relations and gave their arguments against probating the copy short shrift.

The court ruled that the copy of the will could be probated because it was proved by the requisite two witnesses required by the statute—Mr. Pollack and his wife—although she admitted in her testimony that she had never looked at the document she witnessed and had no idea of its contents. Their testimony, with the copy at hand, was sufficient to clearly express Antonio's wishes with respect to the division of his property. Moreover, the terms of this will, according to the court, "recognized a moral, if not legal, obligation" on the part of Antonio "to leave to his two

---

13. The family members who put together *Our Moramarco Family History* emphasized that everyone pitched in on weekends and holidays without pay to work in the family business.

14. *Our Moramarco Family History*, *supra* note 4.

brothers the shares of the estate which they had earned by their labor and other contributions. It was most natural that they should be preferred to the relatives in Italy."

The *Moramarco* case is a sad story when one thinks about the two families divided by economic conditions and a war. And it is evidence of the importance of having a transition in a family business. It states clearly the moral duty that the person controlling the family business has toward members of the family who contribute to that business. When a family member becomes angry with his son or brother, or with her daughter, it is an easy enough matter, although not always advisable, to slam the door or walk out, to cease corresponding, or to cut off an inheritance. There is no legal requirement that one be best friends with one's son, or that one must leave one's property to one's nephews. But when that father or uncle is managing a family business and the son or nephews are minority partners, then a larger duty is owed—a fiduciary duty. Simply put, fiduciaries must exhibit the highest form of trust, fidelity, and confidence, and are expected to act in the best interests of those on whose behalf they are acting, at all times. This was what the court emphasized in the *Moramarco* case: Antonio kept the property in his name, but his brothers and their children had worked hard to help him amass that property and contribute to his success, and he owed a fiduciary duty to the silent and patient partners in his—no, his family's—wine business. This duty took precedence over any formalities that the Italian family members might claim to gain what the court perceived was an undeserved inheritance.

Vignette 3

A Noble Battle—
The Fight for Control of the Château d'Yquem*

One of the most famous and impressive wines from the French Bordeaux region is the sweet, sultry white wine from the Sauternes region produced by the Château d'Yquem. When the wines of Bordeaux were first classified in 1855 into their historic rankings, the Château d'Yquem was given its own special place, a higher ranking than even the highest-rated wines of the Médoc, a "Premium Grand Cru," not just great but a first great.

In good vintages and under the right climatic conditions, the grapes at Château d'Yquem are held on the vines until the very end of the growing season in late October, when they reach a state of perfection—in fact, until they become moldy. But this is no ordinary mold; this is the *botrytis cinerea*, a "noble rot." This mold, when it occurs, causes the grapes to shrivel, leaving sugar-laden fruit with intense, concentrated flavor. The grapes are then hand-picked, selected one-by-one when they have reached their desired ripeness. When the noble rot does not form as needed, however, a nasty fungus may grow instead, something more base, a so-called *"pourriture grise"*—gray rot—and the entire vintage is lost. But in successful years, the resulting wine has been variously described as honeyed, unctuous, nectar-like, liquid gold in a bottle. It is a very expensive wine, selling sometimes for thousands of dollars per bottle—truly a luxurious beverage for a lover of *"produits de luxe."* Which is why Bernard Arnault, the president of the luxury brand conglomerate LVMH (as in Louis Vuitton leather goods, Moët et Chandon Champagne, and Hennessy Cognac, as well as Veuve Cliquot Champagne, Dior couture, and Guerlain perfume), jumped when the chance was offered to acquire this mythic brand.

For almost 400 years, only two families had owned Château

Vignette (continued)

d'Yquem. The Sauvage family received it as a feudal grant in 1593, and the Lur Saluces family gained the rights to it through marriage with a Sauvage daughter in 1785. (The name "Lur Saluces" has been on the bottle's label ever since.)[1] The family and its ownership of Château d'Yquem survived the French Revolution in 1789, the phylloxera epidemic of the nineteenth century, the Nazi occupation during World War II, and all the recent changes in the Bordeaux wine region, including the entree of Robert Parker and the globalization of the wine industry in the latter part of the twentieth century. But it did not survive the familial dispute that led to its transfer in the beginning of the twenty-first century.

The roots of the breakup go back to 1968 and the contested will of the then-proprietor of the Château d'Yquem, the Marquis Bertrand de Lur Saluces. When the Marquis died unmarried and without children (much like Antonio Moramarco, but on a grander scale), his nieces and nephews became the heirs to his estate. In the Marquis's will, the largest holding, approximately 47 percent of the Château d'Yquem, as well as his title, passed to Eugène de Lur Saluces, the eldest son of the Marquis's brother. Much smaller holdings had been or were allocated among some 40 other family members. Shortly before his death, the Marquis had indicated in correspondence a possible intention of changing his will to make Eugène's younger brother, Count Alexandre de Lur Saluces, his heir. But he never did so.[2]

For complicated reasons, Eugène did not take over the management of the winery upon his uncle's death, and his younger brother, Alexandre, assumed the role of general manager. Nine days after their uncle's funeral, the two brothers formalized their arrangement in a secret agreement, in which Alexandre conceded that his brother, Eugène, was the legitimate heir to their uncle's 47 percent share of the family business but Eugène recognized Alexandre as the representative of the Château d'Yquem, with a power of attorney to make all decisions related to its operation. They also apparently agreed to set up a "jointly owned company, with each brother holding a 50 percent

interest, to control the various properties held in the family business, including the Château d'Yquem. The company was never established, but the brothers behaved as if it had been."[3] Eugène retreated to a small apartment in Paris, where he lived a somewhat reclusive life, and Alexandre became the face of the Château d'Yquem, even though he owned outright only a small 7 percent interest (and controlled another 2.2 percent through his son, Bertrand).

For the next 30 years, Alexandre de Lur Saluces lived the good life at d'Yquem, rarely seeing or entertaining the other shareholders (including his brother, Eugène, who never visited the Château), and apparently never treating his cousins or other relatives to the famed wine from the Château in which they shared ownership. He entertained others, however, treating them to lavish fêtes at the Château, dispensing glasses of the delicate wine, served with exquisite foie gras from the region on crisp toast. He was a well-known figure—a true aristocrat— among the Bordeaux wine nobility, and few suspected that the true owner of this family business lived elsewhere. He spent freely on improvements to the property, apparently without consulting other family members, who from time to time raised questions about the appropriateness of certain expenditures or complained about the lack of dividends. As the years went on, these minority owners became more and more vocal in their complaints.[4]

Vignette (continued)

Younger members of the family, who had earned business degrees and who worked in investment houses and for other big companies and therefore knew something about finance, began to voice their displeasure about the lack of transparency in the family business and the dictatorial way in which the winery's affairs were being managed. This eventually broke out into open revolt at a 1992 family meeting at which Alexandre announced a reorganization of the business to create a limited partnership over which he would have absolute control, essentially freezing out the minority shareholders. When they thought they had the votes to block this takeover, Alexandre trumped them, voting Eugène's 47 percent interest under the power of attorney, which, when combined with the 9.2 percent that Alexandre owned or controlled, gave him a majority vote. (Eugène did not attend family business meetings.)

In 1996, Bertrand Hainguerlot, Alexandre's nephew and one of the more dissatisfied shareholders of the younger generation of owners, persuaded the other minority family owners to sell their 37 percent share of the Château d'Yquem to LVMH. They also sought out Eugène de Lur Saluces and eventually convinced him to add some of his shares to the percentage to be acquired by LVMH to increase the acquired interest to more than 50 percent (thereby entitling them to a control premium in the sale). The purchase price paid by LVMH was approximately $100,000 million.[5] Alexandre de Lur Saluces sued.

Under a restraining order issued by the courts in Bordeaux,[6] the family members were prevented from touching any of their newfound wealth gained through the sale until the dispute was resolved, and they also were prevented from visiting the winery. For more than three years Alexandre and LVMH battled in court, first locally in Bordeaux, where public opinion supported Alexandre in what locals viewed as his David-versus-Goliath fight, and then, when Alexandre eventually lost, in the appellate courts in Paris. Finally, in the spring of 1999, worn out by the struggle and possibly realizing that defeat was imminent, Alexandre de Lur Saluces agreed to settle with Bernard Arnault.

(He continued his lawsuit against his brother, Eugène, however, seeking to enforce the 1968 agreement to set up a 50 percent partnership.)

Through the settlement, LVMH acquired a 64 percent interest in the Château d'Yquem, but agreed to bar the other family members from access to the Château and to retain the same management of the winery, with Alexandre as chair of the Board of Directors. The other family owners finally received their millions but could no longer claim any stake in the venerable winery that had been part of their family for so many generations. Alexandre de Lur Saluces remained as the voice and face of the famed Château d'Yquem.

---

* The details In this vignette is extrapolated largely from three sources: WILLIAM ECHIKSON, NOBLE ROT: A BORDEAUX WINE REVOLUTION, W.W. Norton & Co., New York, 2004; contemporary newspaper accounts from both American and French sources, including THE NEW YORK TIMES[7] and SUD-OUEST;[8] and accounts from acquaintances of the author in Bordeaux and Paris who were familiar with the story.

---

1. Official website, Chateau d'Yquem, http://www.yquem.fr/sitehtml/uk/histoire.html.

2. Roger Cohen, *A Chateau Divided: Famed Yquem Riven by Family Feud*, THE NEW YORK TIMES, Jul. 12, 1997, http://www.query.nytimes.com/gst/fullpage.html?res+9EODD1F39F93F931A25754COA901958260&sec=&spon-&pagewanted=all.

3. Roger Cohen, *A Chateau Divided: Famed Yquem Riven by Family Feud*, THE NEW YORK TIMES, Jul. 12, 1997, http://www.query.nytimes.com/gst/fullpage.html?res+9EODD1F39F93F931A25754COA901958260&sec=&spon-&pagewanted=all.

4. Roger Cohen, *A Chateau Divided: Famed Yquem Riven by Family Feud*, THE NEW YORK TIMES, Jul. 12, 1997, http://www.query.nytimes.com/gst/fullpage.html?res+9EODD1F39F93F931A25754COA901958260&sec=&spon-&pagewanted=all.

5. The price was 550 millions of French francs in November 1996 for a 55% interest in the Chateau d'Yquem, *Guide des vins de France: Yquem*, http://www.terroirs-france.com/vin/yquem.html.

6. Les Echos no. 17775 du 17 novembre 1999, p. 11, http://archives.lesechos.fr/archlves/1998/LesEchos/17775-37-ECH.htm.

7. *See*, Roger Cohen, *A Chateau Divided: Famed Yquem Riven by Family Feud*, THE NEW YORK TIMES, Jul. 12, 1997, http://www.query.nytimes.com/gst/fullpage.html?res+9EODD1F39F93F931A25754COA901958260&sec=&spon-&pagewanted=all.

8. *See*, Dominique Richard, *LVMH entre dans le capital*, SUD-OUEST, 15-12-1998, and Didier Ters, *Une si longue attente*, SUD-OUEST, 02-12-1998, http://sudouest.com/archives/v2/archtete.html.

Trouble in the Vineyards— Labor Unrest at the Charles Krug Winery

California Agricultural Labor Relations Board v. C. Mondavi & Sons dba Charles Krug Winery, and United Farm Workers of America, AFL-CIO, Charging Party, Case No. 77-CE-21-S, 4 ALRB No. 52 (1977); *C. Mondavi & Sons dba Charles Krug Winery v. California Agricultural Labor Relations Board*, 1 Civ. No. 44867 (1980)

The Charles Krug Winery is one of the oldest wineries in the Napa Valley. It was founded by Charles Krug, a Prussian immigrant, in 1861, and was renowned at the time for the production of quality varietals in a Germanic style. After Krug's death in 1892, the winery fell into disrepair, but was rescued when it was purchased in 1943 by Cesare Mondavi at the urging of his older son, Robert Mondavi. Robert and his younger brother, Peter, ran the winery together from 1943 until Robert was forced out of the business in 1966. (He subsequently established the Robert Mondavi Winery.) The Charles Krug Winery has been under the ownership and management of Peter Mondavi and his

> *In the 1950s, the Charles Krug Winery was one of the first Napa Valley wineries to open a visitors' center where people could taste samples of Charles Krug-branded wines.*

sons, through the family partnership C. Mondavi & Sons, since that time. The winery has been successful, but from the late 1960s and through the 1980s it struggled financially, partly because of the multimillion-dollar payment the business was required to make to Robert Mondavi in settlement of his lawsuit against his mother, Rosa, and brother, Peter, for the value of his share of the Charles Krug Winery.[1]

The last thing that the Krug Winery needed in the 1970s and 1980s was a costly and protracted labor battle with its workforce just as it was trying to get back on its feet after the lawsuit was settled. And yet that is what it got.

During the initial growth of family wineries in California, the vineyards were tended by the owners and their families, Mexican laborers, and other immigrants. After the United States government instituted the Bracero program in response to labor shortages during and after World War II,[2] vineyards in California were farmed by workers who migrated north from Mexico. Work conditions were hard and pay was kept low. The entry of these low-wage workers into the wine industry led to years of increasing conflict in the vineyards between workers and winery owners.

Seeing the benefits that workers in other industries seemed to enjoy through affiliations with labor unions, and opposed to

---

1. SILER, THE HOUSE OF MONDAVI 287-89.
2. *See* Vignette: "The Vineyard Workers."

the Bracero program, Cesar Chavez, a young man from Arizona working in the Delano area of Central California, set about organizing workers in agricultural industries, including the vineyards owned by the large corporate wineries. In 1965, when workers organized under the AFL-CIO walked out in a strike against grape growers in Delano, Chavez and his organization joined in to support them.[3] The two groups eventually merged to form the United Farm Workers under the umbrella of the AFL-CIO. The strike in Delano lasted for five years, but eventually the union was successful in obtaining contracts with a number of growers, and over time its membership grew.

In 1973, when the E. & J. Gallo Winery signed labor contracts with a rival union, the Teamsters, the UFW workers went out on strike. In addition, they called for a boycott against Gallo products, which eventually gained national recognition.[4] Activist college students of the time, who had first learned to drink wine at concerts and at the beach by passing around gallon jugs of Gallo Hearty Burgundy®, stopped buying wine sold under the Gallo brand name in a sign of solidarity with Chavez and the UFW. It is uncertain what, if any, impact the boycott had. In any event, whether or not as a result of the boycott, the E.& J. Gallo Winery eventually came to the negotiating table with the UFW, and the UFW claimed success.[5]

With the passage of the landmark California Agricultural Labor Relations Act[6] in 1975, the UFW set its sights on organizing workers in the Napa Valley and Sonoma County vineyards. One of the first wineries to be targeted by the union was the Charles Krug Winery. Immediately after passage of the law, the

---

3. United Farm Workers official website: History, http://www.ufw.org.
4. *Id.*
5. *Id.*
6. Cal. Labor Code §§ 1140-1166.3.

Napa Valley–based workers at Krug voted to be represented by the UFW. However, numerous complaints and cross-complaints and hearings before administrative law judges ensued before a contract was finally signed in 1980. After the initial union vote, Krug immediately filed objections (most of which were eventually dismissed) with the newly formed Agricultural Labor Relations Board (ALRB). After hearing and dismissing Krug's charges that the vote had not been properly noticed and that Krug had not been given sufficient time to present an alternative to the union, the ALRB certified the UFW as the exclusive collective bargaining representative of the Krug workers in August, 1977. But Krug refused to bargain with the union and filed further objections with the ALRB, including continued challenges to the certification election. And the UFW filed cross-charges related to Krug's refusal to bargain and alleged mistreatment and discrimination against Krug workers who were UFW representatives, including unlawful dismissal. The administrative law judge ruled in the UFW's favor on many of these complaints, ordering Krug to hire back the affected employees and to bargain in good faith.

But there was still no contract. Krug filed another set of objections and more hearings were held in 1978, 1979, and again in 1980. Each time, Krug's objections—which, according to the ALRB, closely resembled objections that already had been rejected—were dismissed once more. These all related to the validity of the union vote, the lack of notice, and the lack of fair procedures.

In 1980, in light of the "insubstantial nature" of Krug's objections, and considering the UFW's wide margin of victory in the initial representation election, the administrative law judge had concluded, and the ALRB had agreed, that there was no way that Krug could have expected to ever prevail on any of them. After five years of fighting the election, a less tenacious winery might

48

have given up and sat down at the bargaining table with the union. But Krug did not give up. It filed a petition for another review before the ALRB and when this was denied, it appealed the administrative law judge's opinion in the California courts. The California appellate courts refused to hear Krug's challenge, and Krug finally entered into negotiations with the union. A contract with the UFW was signed in 1980.

However, the relationship between the union both during and after the negotiations remained acrimonious, and both the UFW and Krug filed additional petitions before the ALRB. In 1983, a full eight years after the initial union vote, the Board upheld a "make whole" remedy that had been approved by the administrative law judge. This required Krug to reimburse the workers for any loss in pay or other benefits that they had suffered as a result of the long delay from September 1977, when the ALRB first certified the UFW as the exclusive bargaining agent for the Krug workers' contract, and 1980, when the parties finally sat down together to bargain in good faith for a collective bargaining agreement. Because of the newness of all the procedures involving the Agricultural Labor Relations Act, this "make whole" remedy was novel at the time, and Krug was unwilling to accede to it without trying yet one more appeal. Accordingly, it filed a number of challenges in continued proceedings before the ALRB, all of which were heard and eventually dismissed.

In the ensuing years, peace and quiet did not come to the Charles Krug Winery. There were reports of confrontations, pickets, and other unrest, including a labor lockout in the early 2000s, which created an angry and hostile environment.[7]

Life has not been easy for the unions, either. In the early years of the twenty-first century, there has been a backlash

---

7. SILER, *supra* note 2 at 288-89.

against the UFW and its presence in the Napa Valley and Sonoma County, not just by the winery owners but by the union members themselves. For some years between the time of its early successes in the 1970s and 1980s, contracts with the UFW were renewed as their expiration dates approached. And in 1994, the UFW successfully unionized the farm workers at the Gallo Winery in Sonoma County.[8] But the balance has recently shifted. In June 2007, Gallo of Sonoma vineyard workers, who had been unionized only a decade before, voted to oust the UFW.[9] And in July 2007, workers at Kunde Winery in Sonoma County also voted to reject the union.[10]

This shift has affected once again the tenuous relationship between the UFW and management at the Charles Krug Winery. In late 2005, the UFW notified Krug that it intended to extend the existing contract with Krug, as the parties had not yet come to terms on the most recent renewal and the contract was set to expire on December 31 of that year. Krug rejected the contract extension and, in January 2006, notified the UFW that it was going out of the vineyard management business and was turning its winery and vineyard operations over to a "land manager," an independent company that would not be using any union labor.[11] The union protested this move as a subterfuge to kick out the union, in violation of the Agricultural Labor Relations Act.[12] In

8. *Gallo, Heat, Unions*, RURAL MIGRATION NEWS, July, 2005, Vol. II No. 3, http://migration.ucdavis.edu/rmn/more.php?id=1041_0_3_0.

9. Kevin McCallum and Angelica Marin, *Gallo Workers Toss Out UFW*, SANTA ROSA PRESS DEMOCRAT, Tues., June 26, 2007, http://www1.pressdemocrat.com/article/2007 0626/NEWS/706260333/1033/NEWS01.

10. Kevin McCallum and Angelica Marin, *UFW Loses Second Local Vineyard*, SANTA ROSA PRESS DEMOCRAT, Fri., July 27, 2007, http://www1.pressdemocrat.com/article/2007 0727/NEWS/707270409.

11. Julissa McKinnon, *Krug Workers Want New Contract*, ST. HELENA STAR, Thurs., June 8, 2006, http://www.sthelenastar.com/articles/2006/06/08/news/local/iq-3465413.txt.

12. CAL. LABOR CODE §§ 1153(e).

July 2006, in accordance with its earlier announcement, the Charles Krug Winery made its move, firing the 36 unionized workers in its winery and severing its ties with the union.[13] The UFW then challenged the firings with the ALRB, and, in the summer of 2006, it also announced a boycott of the Charles Krug and C. K. Mondavi labeled wines. In June, 2007, the ALRB announced that it would bring formal charges against the Charles Krug Winery for violations of the Agricultural Labor Relations Act; and in April 2008, the workers were reinstated with back pay.[14]

The Napa Valley has always seemed such a bucolic place, but underneath the surface, not all is well. It seems that peace remains elusive in the Valley, at least on the labor front, particularly for the Charles Krug Winery.

---

13. Carlos Villatoro, *Krug Defends Decision, Says Union has not Responded to Bargaining Efforts*, NAPA VALLEY REGISTER, Sun., July 9, 2006, http://www.napavalley register.com/articles/2006/07/09/news/local/iq-3491856.txt.

14. United Farm Workers official website, *Charles Krug Mondavi Wine Boycott is Over*, http://www.ufw.org/page.php?menu=research&inc=history/01.html. *See*, Kerana Todorov, *UFW Workers Return to Krug*, NAPA VALLEY REGISTER, Sat., April 5, 2008, http://www.napavalleyregister.com/articles/2008/04/05/news/local/doc47fe84e867d94 1601317.txt.

Vignette

The Vineyard Workers

The history of immigration into the United States is reflected in the history of wine production, especially in California. The earliest vineyard workers were the Native Americans who lived and worked at the missions established by the Franciscan friars, from San Diego in the South to Sonoma in the North. Among their duties would have been the care of the Mission grapes planted by the friars and the making of the wine. As wine production expanded in California in the nineteenth century, the mission labor was augmented by that of workers resident in California and those migrating north from Mexico. (Initially, California was part of the Spanish land holdings from southern Mexico to an area north of Sonoma and the Napa Valley.)

From the time of their first immigration in the 1850s to work on the railroads and in the gold mines, Chinese laborers also worked in the wine industry. For example, the famous caves at Sonoma's Buena Vista Winery were carved out of the hills by Chinese workers.[1] Several hundred thousand had arrived and worked in the fields until the passage of the Oriental Exclusion Act of 1882.[2] Then the Chinese workers were replaced by Italian immigrants, newly arrived from East Coast cities, who found the California semi-desert landscape to be reminiscent of their homeland. Many of these workers were able to gradually build their own businesses, as saloon owners, as grape growers, and as winemakers. It is no surprise that some of the most famous names in the California wine industry today, such as Gallo and Mondavi, are descendants of Italian immigrants.

As a result of the Mexican Revolution in 1910, Mexican workers continued to migrate into the United States, seeking work in the fields. They freely went back and forth across the border, performing the seasonal work required in the vineyards until 1924, when the Border Patrol was established by Act of Congress.[3] This changed the immigration status of many

immigrants by limiting the numbers of persons of different nationalities who could legally immigrate to the United States.

During Prohibition, even though many wineries shut down, the grape industry thrived (as large quantities of fruit were sent East for home winemakers), and Italian and Mexican laborers worked long hours for relatively low wages. With the onset of the Great Depression and the crash of the grape market at Repeal in 1933, jobs became scarce. The problem for workers was exacerbated by the arrival in California of migrant workers from the Oklahoma and Texas dust bowls, those epitomized in John Steinbeck's novel of the period, *The Grapes of Wrath*. This situation changed dramatically with World War II; suddenly, just as the wine industry was attempting to revitalize itself after the dual blows of Prohibition and the Depression, it was faced with a manpower shortage.

The United States, in need of migrant workers not just for the vineyards but for its entire agricultural industry, negotiated a labor agreement with Mexico in the summer of 1942, giving rise to the first Bracero program, which allowed Mexican farmworkers to enter the country on a short-term basis to perform agricultural work.[4] Under the Bracero Agreement, Mexicans entering the United States enjoyed guarantees of transportation, living

Vignette (continued)

expenses, and repatriation established under Mexican Federal Labor Law.[5] The Agreement also established that Mexicans entering the United States under its terms would not suffer discriminatory acts of any kind.[6] The Bracero program ended in 1947, but was revived in 1951 and continued until 1964. Growers liked the program because it assured them of a pool of legal, inexpensive labor to meet seasonal harvesting and vineyard maintenance demands. But organized labor leaders hated the program because they believed that it depressed wages for all winery workers. One reason that Cesar Chavez gained early success in organizing workers in California and Arizona was a general dislike among workers of the Bracero Agreement. Once the program was ended in 1964, Chavez launched his first strike against the Delano Vineyards in California's Central Valley.[7]

1. PINNEY, A HISTORY OF WINE IN AMERICA 243.

2. An Act to Execute Certain Treaty Stipulations Relating to Chinese, Acts of 1882 (47th Congress), ch. 126.

3. Immigration Act of 1924, also known as the Johnson-Reed Act, Act of May 26, 1924, *as amended* 45 STAT. 1009 (May 29, 1928).

4. The Agreement was finalized on April 26, 1943.

5. Article 29.

6. Agreement General Provision 21, in accordance with Executive Order No. 8802, June 25, 1941.

7. United Farm Workers official website, http://www.ufw.org.

The Battle of the Giants:
When Is a Contract Not a Contract?

Kendall-Jackson Winery, Ltd. v. Branson and Wirtz Corporation dba Judge & Dolph, Ltd., 212 F.3d 995 (7th Cir. 2000)

I magine that you have come into your inheritance or sold your stock options and can now live your dream of setting up a small artisanal winery in the Napa Valley, joining the dozens of others who have opened their doors in the last two decades. Wine has been your hobby for many years, and you know how to make a good product. You have a business plan, and your first goal is to get your product into local retail shops and restaurants. From there, as your inventory grows, you hope to sell in other metropolitan areas where wine enthusiasts live, such as New York City, Chicago, New Orleans, and Miami. But you learn very quickly that you cannot do that without having a distributor in each state where these cities are located who will be willing to take on the sale and marketing of your product. It is not just that using a distribution network is desirable for quick market entry; it is mandated by law in any state that has—as many do—a three-tier system for the sale and marketing of wine: the producer sells to the wholesaler, who in turn sells to the retailer. And the retailer sells to the consumer. So you find a distributor, and then your adventure really begins.

The business dealings between a distributor and a supplier in any industry are generally determined by the contract that they have in place. Until recently, in the wine industry, where distributors were mostly small, family-owned local businesses, many of these contracts were oral and depended to some extent on a good personal relationship between the parties. In more recent times, as both wine businesses and distributors have grown larger, the contracts are written and specify the payment terms, whether or not the distributor is entitled to an exclusive territory, and also under what circumstances the supplier can terminate the agreement. In some states, these terms negotiated between the parties will govern. But in what are known as "franchise states," the contract terms will be superseded by other rules.

This complicates the ability of a small winery to market its wines. The dynamics have shifted so that you are no longer dealing with a small, locally-owned distributor. Now it is more likely that your small winery must deal on uneven terms with large distributors who have significant control over the marketing decisions involving your wine, including whether to take it in the first place, how much promotion to afford it, and where to sell it. It is difficult enough for a new winery to gain entry into what has become a very crowded market if it is unable to find a distributor willing to invest the money into marketing its wines. But some states also have in place franchise laws[1] that create additional barriers to this market entry. Franchise laws and so-called exclusive dealing laws impose restrictions on the ability of a winery to

---

1. *See* Vignette: "The Rise of the Distribution Industry—Post-Prohibition."

use more than one distributor in a market and to terminate a contract where the distribution relationship has gone sour. Because of the obstacles to termination imposed by these laws, producers often find themselves locked into a seemingly never-ending contract once distribution begins. And because of the political power that the wholesalers industry wields in virtually every state, instead of softening these laws or eliminating them entirely, as the need for them arguably has ceased in light of changing market conditions, state legislatures frequently have bowed to the pressure of wholesalers' lobbying groups and have in recent years strengthened the restrictions in these laws.

A good example of this was the Illinois Wine and Spirits Industry Fair Dealing Act of 1999.[2] This statute made it unlawful for a supplier of alcoholic beverages, such as a winery, to cancel or substantially alter any distribution arrangement without good cause. "Good cause" was defined in a very restrictive way that would make most contracts virtually evergreen. A number of suppliers, including Kendall-Jackson Winery—a large California-based winery that had made so-called "fighting varietals" (inexpensive cork-finished varietal wines such as Chardonnay or Cabernet Sauvignon) popular in the 1980s—decided to terminate existing distributorships before the law took effect. Their goal was to give themselves a chance to bid out their distribution contracts and to put better pricing and other terms into place before being locked into disadvantageous long-term agreements in Illinois. But the statute went further: it also authorized the Illinois Liquor Control Commission to order suppliers to continue to use the same distributors, on the same terms and at the same prices, even if the existing contracts had permitted termination for convenience (without cause).[3]

---

2. 815 Ill. Liquor Control Stats. (ILCS) 725/1–725/99.
3. 815 ILCS 725/35 (c)(2).

As soon as the Act went into effect, several distributors asked the Commission to order suppliers to resume dealings under the old contracts that the suppliers had attempted to terminate before the law took effect. On this request, the Commission issued orders directing the suppliers to reinstate their prior contracts with the distributors.

Three suppliers, Kendall-Jackson Winery, Jim Beam Brands, and Sutter Home Winery, sued in federal district court in Illinois, arguing that the Illinois Act violated the Contracts Clause of the U.S. Constitution.[4] That clause provides: "No State shall . . . pass any . . . Law impairing the Obligations of Contracts. . . ." The suppliers argued that the Illinois Act unconstitutionally deprived them of significant rights, including the right to freely choose their distributors and to negotiate prices for services, which they had held under their prior contracts, before passage of the Illinois law. The district court issued a preliminary injunction against the Commission at the request of the suppliers, preventing the Commission's orders from taking effect, on the basis that the Illinois statute probably violated the Contracts Clause. The suppliers then dropped their old distributors, who appealed to the Seventh Circuit Court of Appeals. But the Commission did not appeal.

This created a problem for the distributors, because the injunction had been issued against the *Commission*, not against the *distributors*. For the distributors, this seemed to be a distinction without a difference because, they argued, they were the ones who were deprived of the benefits of the statute solely because the Commission hadn't bothered to appeal. They also claimed that the Act did not change Illinois law anyway, so the suppliers' contracts had not actually been altered, and thus there

---

4. U.S. CONST. Art. I, Sec. 10(1).

was no Contracts Clause problem. Under prior law, they maintained, it would have been unlawful to modify or terminate a liquor distribution agreement in the absence of good cause, because Illinois law imposes a general duty of good faith and fair dealing in all contracts.

That's too bad, the appellate court essentially told them. The court clearly was not impressed with the distributors' arguments. In fact, they seemed to be particularly pleased to take these same arguments and to turn them against the distributors. Well, the court said, if Illinois had such a general rule applicable to contracts, which they doubted, then the distributors should go ahead and file their own breach of contract actions against the suppliers in Illinois state court, instead of trying to intercede into the suppliers' case against the state. State court was where they belonged and that is where they should go, the court told them. If they were proved correct in a state court action, then they would not need the "protection" afforded to them by the unconstitutional Illinois law anyway.

"If the distributors are wrong, however," the Court continued, "then it is hard to avoid the district court's conclusion that [the Act] has serious Constitutional problems, because it dramatically reallocates rights under contracts that predate the legislation, and again the distributors do not have much to gain by this appeal."

In other words, they were the wrong people in the wrong court trying to defend the wrong law. And if they disagreed, they also could go to state court and obtain an order forcing the Commission to appeal the district court's injunction.

The Rise of the Distribution Industry— Post-Prohibition

When you go into a store to buy a bottle of wine, as you scan over the selections on the shelves, you probably don't think about the logistical trail that the bottle took to get from the winery into the store. Particularly if you treat a bottle of wine like any other consumer item, such as a book or a dress, as you pay for the item at the cash register, you would not note any difference among them. But there is a difference. As a general rule, there are no regulations prohibiting dress manufacturers, for example, from selling at retail the clothing they make, or from opening up a chain of shops in which to place their own merchandise. And there is no regulation that prevents them from bypassing distributors entirely and selling their merchandise directly into retailers' establishments. But there is a wide range of regulations in many states that prevent producers of wine from selling their product at retail, except possibly from the winery premises. And other requirements prevent the producer from distributing its own product.

When the Twenty-first Amendment repealed Prohibition in 1933, rather than permit the production and sale of alcoholic beverages to become unregulated, and fearful of the criminal elements (in the form of organized crime) that had entered the alcoholic beverage industry during Prohibition, most states adopted some form of system to regulate the business. The most favored of these was the so-called "three-tier" system of producers, wholesalers (distributors), and retailers. Under this system, in its most rigid form, no owner in one tier can invest in another. This prohibition, for example, prevents a winery from owning an off-premises retail liquor shop. One of the consequences of the three-tier system was the investment of power into the liquor distribution industry. To this day, to place their product into retail shops and restaurants in many states, wineries depend on the efforts of distributors licensed in those various states. Most wine sales in the United States go through wholesalers before reaching the ultimate consumer, and the top five distribution companies in the United States represent 43 percent of total wine and spirit sales, according to the Wine Institute, a California winery owner lobbying group.[1]

As an additional layer in some states are so-called "franchise laws." These laws were put in place at the end of Prohibition to ensure that a strong legal distributorship network would develop (to replace the illegal network that grew up during Prohibition under the auspices of organized crime). The original and stated purpose of franchise laws was to protect liquor distributors, who were frequently "mom and pop" operations, from capricious and unfair treatment by the then large and powerful beverage manufacturers, such as distillers and brewers, and to make these start-up companies whole from the significant economic hardship that could result from the termination of a distribution contract before its natural expiration. Because distributors make significant up-front investments into the acquisition of inventory and in marketing the alcoholic beverages of a particular producer, these costs are not recouped if the relationship is prematurely terminated. As adopted in many three-tier states, franchise laws restrict the ability of wineries and distributors to freely negotiate the terms of their business dealings. The rights and responsibilities of the parties are imposed under the law and override any contrary provisions that the parties may agree to. In keeping with the goals of these laws, in a franchise state, for example, the business relationship between the winery and the distributor frequently cannot be terminated except for "good cause," and then only if certain conditions are met.

In recent years, however, as the distribution industry has consolidated, the potential hardships against which franchise and exclusive territory laws were enacted are less evident, and in fact it is often the small wine producer who faces hardship. There are simply too few wholesalers with whom producers can work.[2] The

Vignette (continued)

dynamics have shifted so that it is now more likely that small, family-owned wineries must deal on uneven terms with large distribution corporations that enjoy significant market clout, and that, to add insult to injury, enjoy statutory protection. And in recent years, lobbying groups for the distribution industry have been able to strengthen franchise laws and to ensure the continued viability of the three-tier network. For example, after the U.S. Supreme Court decision in *Granholm v. Heald*[3]—which wine industry representatives hoped would open the doors to allow wineries to make Internet sales and to direct-ship not just to retailers and restaurants but also to consumers' homes— the wholesalers' industry has been able, in several states, to influence legislation that actually rolled back the ability of wineries to direct-ship. For example, after a 2005 court decision in Virginia that prevented in-state wineries from shipping to retailers and restaurants, thus limiting those wineries' ability to bypass distributors, wholesalers blocked legislation that would have opened up direct shipment by any winery, whether in-state or out-of-state.[4]

---

1. MFK Research Report on Economic Impact of California Wine 2006 (Update January 2007), sponsored by the Wine Institute, p. 14, *available at* http://www.wineinstitute.org/files/mfk_ca_econ_reporto6_0.pdf.

2. In 1984, there were over 1,600 licensed wine distributors in the United States. From 1990 to 2000, the number of wine wholesalers and distributors had declined by more than 50% as a result of consolidation in the industry. MFK Research Report at 14.

3. *See* Case 9.

4. Virginia repealed its statute prohibiting direct sales to Virginia consumers in 2003. A law was finally passed in 2008 (effective April 17, 2008) that sets up a low-cost, state-subsidized distribution company—the Virginia Winery Distribution Company—to act as a wholesaler on behalf of small in-state wineries, to allow them a means to get their product back into restaurants and retail shops.

Blood Is Not Thicker than Wine— The Gallo Family Feud

E. & J. Gallo Winery v. Gallo Cattle Co.,
967 F.2d 1280 (9th Cir. 1992)[1]

T he saga of the court battle between the Gallo brothers is a tale worthy of a television miniseries. As the court itself stated, the lawsuit arose out of "a tortuous family history apparently involving sibling rivalry on a grand scale." It is the story of two closely knit older brothers and a younger one who, depending on whose side was doing the telling, either tried to take unfair advantage of the name his older brothers had worked for over 30 years to make famous or was cheated out of his inheritance while he was under their guardianship as a young boy. The story is clouded in mystery, partly because the family understandably did not wish to publicize some of the less salubrious facts, especially those surrounding their father's possibly crimi-

---

1. Disclaimer: the author was a director in the law firm that represented Joseph Gallo and the Gallo Cattle Company before the district court in Modesto in the defense of the trademark infringement lawsuit and the counterclaim. She had no involvement in the litigation, and the description of the dispute and the case is based solely on the facts as described in the case and public newspaper and other published accounts.

nal activities during Prohibition (bootlegging) and their parents' untimely deaths, and partly because the facts do not fully correspond with the history created by Ernest and Julio Gallo, the older brothers, to explain the founding of their winery. As told, this family legend is a classic rags-to-riches story of two orphaned brothers, left destitute during the Great Depression after the sudden deaths of their parents, who taught themselves how to make wine by reading a University of California pamphlet in the basement of their local library, and founded a small winery with their only assets in the world: $900, and $5,000 in borrowed funds.[2] This winery grew to become the biggest and one of the most profitable wineries in the United States, the E. & J. Gallo Winery.

From the facts that were brought out in the lawsuit between the winery on the one side and the younger brother on the other, the story is much more complicated and perhaps darker. Ernest and Julio Gallo, owners of the E. & J. Gallo Winery, sued their younger brother, Joseph Gallo, for trademark infringement because he was using the famous "Gallo" name on cheeses. Joseph's version of events was different. He claimed that he had worked hard as a young man in the winery business that had been started by their parents before their deaths, and his brothers cheated him out of his rightful inheritance while he was still a minor and they were his legal guardians. Then, to further humiliate him, they sued him when he set himself up in a different line of business (dairy farming) and tried to market cheese—not wine—under his own name, Joseph Gallo.

Ernest, Julio, and Joseph Gallo, Jr. were the sons of Joseph Gallo, Sr. and his wife, Susie, who had emigrated to California

---

2. W. Blake Gray and Steve Rubinstein, *Winemaker Ernest Gallo dies at age 97*, SAN FRANCISCO CHRONICLE, Tues., March 6, 2007, http://www.sfgate.com/cgi-bin/article.cgi?f=/c/a/2007/03/06/MNG2POGHIR13.DTL

from Italy in the early 1900s. Ernest was born in 1909, Julio in 1910, and Joseph almost 10 years later in 1919. The Gallo parents ran a boarding house and a saloon near Modesto, California, serving bulk wine that they kept in kegs in their basement. There was no evidence that they made their own wine, although the kegs were imprinted with the word "GALLO." During Prohibition, they invested in vineyards and grew grapes that they shipped east for the home wine-making market. According to the court record, Joseph Gallo had a "brush with the law" due to involvement in bootlegging. He was never arrested, however.

The older Gallo brothers—Ernest and Julio—became involved in the family grape-shipping business in the 1920s. Shortly before Repeal, at the start of the Great Depression, the grape market crashed, prices dropped precipitously, and the family finances were ruined. On June 21, 1933, according to the case history, Joseph Sr. shot his wife, Susie, and then killed himself.[3] Susie left a holographic will leaving one-third of her estate, which consisted of stock and other property, to each of her three sons. Joseph Sr. left no will. The accountings of the parents' estates listed all their assets but showed no wine business, although it did name the E. & J. Gallo Winery as a creditor of the estate. This was a partnership that Ernest Gallo listed on his reports to the probate court as having been formed between the two brothers after their parents' deaths. He obtained a court order authorizing him to carry on the family business of "raising grapes and other crops."[4] Prohibition ended December 5, 1933,

---

3. *See,* Frank J. Prial, *Wine Talk: A Feud and A Book Unplug the Cork on the Gallo Empire,* THE NEW YORK TIMES, April 14, 1993, http://query.nytimes.com/gst/fullpage.html?res=9FOCE7D91F3AF937A25757COA965958260.

4. It is worth noting that if the Gallo parents had operated a winery during Prohibition, as Joseph later claimed, it would likely not have been shown as such on the list of assets of the estate but disguised as something else, because making wine without a permit for medicinal or sacramental wine would have been a clandestine, illegal activity and there is no evidence that either Joseph Sr. or Susie Gallo had such a permit.

In December 1933, after Repeal, the E. & J.
Gallo Winery made its first shipments of
Gallo-branded wine.

---

and on that day the E. & J. Gallo Winery began shipping wine out of California in barrels marked "GALLO."[5]

Ernest and Julio became the legal guardians of Joseph Jr., who was 12 years old at the time of their parents' deaths. According to the court, they were not as meticulous as they could have been at keeping accurate paperwork and making accountings. In 1936, they obtained a court order authorizing them to sell shares of stock that Joseph had inherited from his mother, but they then lent the proceeds from the sale to the winery without the court's authorization. In 1941, after Joseph became an adult, he engaged a lawyer and filed an action against his brothers for their misuse of those shares of stock for the investment into the winery business. The court awarded him $20,000 in settlement.

From their small start in 1933, Ernest and Julio grew their winery business, first selling wine in barrels and tank cars to wholesalers who bottled it under their own trademarks, and then later bottling the wine themselves, using the "GALLO" trademark. Joseph worked as a boy in the winery business, but when he became an adult, he started his own business as a cattle rancher and farmer. In the meantime, the E. & J. Gallo Winery continued to grow and prosper. In 1942, it obtained its first registered trademark using the word "GALLO." By the early 1960s,

---

5. Tony Lima and Norma Schroder, *Ernest Gallo, 1909-2007: A Life in Wine,* JOURNAL OF WINE ECONOMICS, Vol. 2 No. 2, Fall 2007, 115, http://www.wine-economics. org/journal/content/volume2/number2/FullTexts/wineeconomics_Lima.pdf.

Ernest and Julio had established distribution of wine sold under the GALLO brand in all major U.S. markets.

Independently of the Gallo wine business, in the 1940s, another company, "Gallo Salame"—not related to the Gallo family—began producing salami and other prepared meat products, which were sold at wholesale to delicatessens. In 1959, Gallo Salame began selling its products directly to consumers and in the 1970s added a cheese and salami combination pack to its product line. In 1970, it obtained a registered trademark for these products under the name "GALLO," and the E. & J. Gallo Winery sued Gallo Salame for trademark infringement and dilution. The case settled in 1983 with Gallo Salame assigning its trademark to the winery, and the winery licensing back to Gallo Salame the right to use the mark "GALLO SALAME" on its meat and related products.

Meanwhile, Joseph Gallo's cattle and farming operations also prospered. In his ventures, he used his name, "Joseph Gallo," as a trade name. He also purchased a vineyard and sold grapes (including, apparently, to the E. & J. Gallo Winery) under the trade name "Joseph Gallo Vineyards." In 1955 he established the Gallo Cattle Company, a partnership that raised and sold dairy cattle. In the late 1970s, the Gallo Cattle Company established a dairy, and in 1983 it entered the cheese business. It initially sold the cheese at wholesale in large blocks that were then cut down, packaged, and sold under various marks. But by 1984, Joseph had begun selling packages of cheese in retail markets, labeled with a trademark consisting of his name, "JOSEPH GALLO," and accompanied by a bucolic scene of dairy cows and a barn.

When his brothers learned that he was selling this cheese in retail markets, they sent him a letter advising him that he was infringing on the winery's trademarks. They also advised Gallo

Salame Company, which insisted that the winery either stop Joseph from using the name "GALLO" on his cheeses or have him sign a licensing agreement for the use of the name (with a likely sharing of royalty payments between the winery and Gallo Salame). The brothers were unable to come to terms, and on April 17, 1986, the winery sued Gallo Cattle Company as well as Joseph Gallo for trademark infringement and dilution.

Joseph was personally affronted by this suit. There were two flames that fed his anger. First, he believed that his brothers were trying to prevent him from using his own name—a name to which he felt just as entitled as they—on his own products. Second, news articles recounted his frustration at not having shared fully in the success of the winery, which he believed to have been a venture first envisioned and perhaps founded by his father, Joseph Sr.[6]

Joseph countersued. He asserted that his parents had founded the winery as early as 1909 and had continued operations, albeit clandestinely, throughout Prohibition. He claimed also that Ernest and Julio had breached their fiduciary duty to him, and engaged in deceit and fraud, in their conduct of his guardianship. The proceedings were held in Modesto, California, the home of the E. & J. Gallo Winery. Joseph's lawyers failed to get the trial venue moved to a more neutral location. The winery moved to dismiss Joseph's counterclaims and won. And the court also issued an injunction, permanently barring Joseph from using the "GALLO" mark on retail cheese packages or on any advertising

---

6. *See, e.g.*, Frank J. Prial, *Wine Talk: A Feud and A Book Unplug the Cork on the Gallo Empire*, THE NEW YORK TIMES, April 14, 1993, http://query.nytimes.com/gst/fullpage.html?res=9F0CE7D913AF937A25757C0A965958260; *see also*, Valerie J. Nelson, *Joseph Gallo, 87: California Dairy Magnate Lost Legal Fight with his Winemaker Brothers*, LOS ANGELES TIMES, page B-6, Feb. 22, 2007, http://articles/latimes.com/2007/feb/22/local/me-gallo22, and Andrew Gumbel, *The Curse of the House of Gallo*, THE INDEPENDENT (Food and Drink), Sat., March 3, 2007, http://www.independent.co.uk/life-style/food-and-drink/features/the-curse-of-the-house-of-gallo-438587.html.

for the cheese. Joseph moved for a new trial on the basis that the trial judge had once been a partner in the local law firm that had represented the winery in its trademark suit against Gallo Salame. The judge ruled that this challenge came too late. Joseph then appealed to the Ninth Circuit Court of Appeals. The appellate court affirmed the lower court's decisions, both rejecting Joseph's countersuit for fraud and breach of fiduciary duty and barring Joseph from using the "GALLO" mark on his cheese.

In considering Joseph's claim that he had been cheated out of his inheritance, Joseph had presented only circumstantial evidence that the winery was part of the Gallo parents' estate. For example, Joseph Sr. had expressed publicly an intent to start a winery after Repeal; Ernest and Julio used grapes from their father's vineyard to make their wine; they sold the wine under the same "GALLO" trademark that their parents had put on the barrels of wine that they kept in the basement of their saloon before Prohibition; and, perhaps most important, Ernest and Julio had represented in several trademark applications (to demonstrate first and continuous use) that the winery was a continuation of their father's business and that the "GALLO" mark had been used initially by Joseph Sr. on wine since the early 1900s.[7]

But the appellate court did not want to delve into what it considered to be ancient history. All this had happened so long ago that the trial court judge simply had had no way of telling what was truth and what was not, and the appellate court agreed that it was better not to revisit that issue. In addition, Joseph had received a $20,000 payment in settlement of his earlier action against his brothers for misuse of the stock he had inherited from his mother, and he had not presented "smoking gun" facts

7. Andrew Gumbel, *The Curse of the House of Gallo*, THE INDEPENDENT (Food and Drink), Sat., March 3, 2007, http://www.independent.co.uk/life-style/food-and-drink/features/the-curse-of-the-house-of-gallo-438587.html.

sufficient to raise a likelihood of winning on a fraud claim. (Although, if Joseph's claims were true and his brothers had hidden the winery assets in their accountings to the probate court, $20,000—which was for something entirely different: using stock gains to finance the winery—would seem a small payment for deprivation of an asset that ultimately became a multimillion-dollar business.) But Joseph's claims were not deemed strong enough to allow him to move forward, and he was not given his chance to present his evidence at a trial.

On the other hand, the court found without a doubt that Joseph's use of his name on retail packages of cheese infringed on the winery's trademarks and constituted unfair competition under the Lanham Trademark Act,[8] even though Joseph had raised several arguments against the injunction that he had thought persuasive.

First, courts generally are reluctant to prevent a person from using his own name as a trademark, especially where that person had made no attempt to confuse the public. Moreover, Joseph argued that the GALLO mark was not a strong or distinctive mark because it was also Ernest's and Julio's personal name. The court disagreed. While acknowledging that trademark law gives greater protection to marks that are distinctive and that personal names are not inherently distinctive, they can nevertheless be treated as strong marks when they have acquired *secondary* meaning—that is, in the consumer's mind, the mark becomes associated with a particular source. The court found the "GALLO" mark to be one that had acquired such a secondary meaning because of its "widespread national public recognition," as well as the winery's long-term efforts to advertise, promote, and protect its mark.

---

8. 15 U.S.C. §§1125 et seq. *See* Vignette: "Trademark Law in Brief."

Second, Joseph had argued that even if the "GALLO" brand had acquired secondary meaning, that meaning was related to wine and related products, but not cheese. Accordingly, protection should not be extended to other product fields where the winery had no activity and where there was no likelihood of consumer confusion. He maintained that there was an insufficient connection between *wine* and *cheese*. However, the court refused to accept this argument, finding that wine and cheese are "complimentary products frequently served together in wine and cheese tasting parties." The court also recognized that Gallo Salame Company, which had a license to sell salami and other meat products under the "GALLO" name, sold salami and cheese in a combination pack. There was, therefore, a *likelihood* of consumer confusion, even if the winery had not presented evidence of actual confusion.

Furthermore, the court found that Joseph was, in fact, culpable of engaging in unfair competition by trying to capitalize on the fame of his brothers' winery. The winery had presented evidence that when Joseph had first entered the cheese business, selling wholesale, his brothers had warned him that they would not want him to use the Gallo name on the products if he sold them at retail. When he decided to enter the retail market, a consultant advised him that the products tested more favorably for consumer recognition when he used his surname, "Gallo," on the packages. It was after receiving that advice that Joseph had decided to add his name, Joseph Gallo, to the label. This was sufficient for the court to find against Joseph.

In the end, Joseph Gallo did not suffer irreparable financial harm from the court's judgment. Although he could no longer use GALLO or JOSEPH GALLO as trademarks for the retail sale of cheese, he was permitted to continue to use JOSEPH GALLO as a trademark on wholesale packages of cheese, and he was allowed to use "Gallo Cattle Co." and "Joseph Gallo Farms" as trade names. The injunction was silent as to products other than cheese. Joseph changed the name on his retail cheeses to "JOSEPH'S" and the products continued to sell. However, in terms of a personal toll, the court's judgment devastated the younger Gallo brother. He was humiliated. He was not able to forget that his brothers had delivered this final blow, depriving him of the free use of his own family name and suing him, publicly accusing him of unfair competition. By all accounts, he did not speak to his brothers again, and all three died without any public demonstration of repairing the rift in the family bond that this bitter lawsuit caused.[9]

---

9. Michael J. de la Merced, *Joseph E. Gallo, 87, Brother Who Left Wine for Cheese, Dies*, THE NEW YORK TIMES, Feb. 23, 2007, http://www.nytimes.com/2007/02/23/business/23gallo.html.

The Judgment of Paris and One Case That Settled in an "Accord"

*Stag's Leap Wine Cellars
versus Stags' Leap Winery*

On the east side of the Napa Valley is an outcrop of cliffs known as "Stags Leap." According to the legend of the Wappo tribe, hunters were pursuing a mighty stag through the eastern hills, drawing him closer and closer to the cliffs, where they hoped to take him. But rather than allow itself to be trapped, the stag rushed forward toward the edge of the cliff and leaped in the air, reaching the other side and vanishing. The place was memorialized as "Stags Leap."

On May 24, 1976, a blind tasting took place in Paris, with a panel of judges made up exclusively of French wine experts, matching California wines against top French wines. No one doubted the outcome. The entire purpose of the tasting was simply to introduce some of the new wines coming out of California to the broader wine world and to see how they would fare compared to the best-known French wines. Of course, everyone knew that French wines would dominate.[1] Just a few years before in 1970, at a dinner I had attended in Bordeaux, an American friend from South Carolina had summed up the opinion that not only the French but also many Americans held of California wines at the time, when she declaimed that *"les vins californiens sont dégoûtants"* (California wines are disgusting). Her Bordeaux hosts, of course, nodded their heads in agreement, even though none of them had ever tasted a good California wine and were merely relying on past reputation and their own admittedly biased opinions. At the time, I assumed that she was probably right, although I had no point of comparison.

After comparing several California Chardonnays against

Vignette (continued)

French wines made from the Chardonnay grape (from the Burgundy region of France) and California Cabernet Sauvignons against first and other classified-growth red Bordeaux wines, the nine French judges surprised everyone—not least themselves—by ranking the California wines higher than the French. Among the whites, California's Chateau Montelena Chardonnay was ranked the highest, Chalone Vineyard's came in third, and Spring Mountain Vineyard fourth. When the reds were evaluated, the 1973 Stag's Leap Wine Cellars S.L.V. Cabernet Sauvignon—the winery's first vintage produced with grapes from vines that were barely three years old—was judged the best. Bordeaux's Château Mouton-Rothschild was second, and Château Haut-Brion was third.[2] The only journalist at the tasting was a *TIME* magazine correspondent who was a surprise witness to history in the making. He sent in his report and the impact was immediate.[3] This news fundamentally transformed how California wines were viewed worldwide.

How had this happened? How had wines that had been disparaged just a few years before, and in effect for the past

100 years, and produced by novice winemakers out of grapes grown on new vines, managed to win in a competition against the best of the best Bordeaux and Burgundy wines?

Stag's Leap Wine Cellars was a new and relatively unknown winery even in the Napa Valley until that famous 1976 Paris tasting. It had been founded just a few years before by Warren Winiarski, a former political science lecturer from the University of Chicago, who had apprenticed at several of Napa Valley's premier vineyards, including the Robert Mondavi Winery. In 1970, he acquired a small vineyard on the east side of the Napa Valley, in the Stags Leap area, and began producing his own wines.[4]

Below the cliffs in the little valley another winery, called Stags' Leap Winery, is located. A winery had originally been situated in the same location in the 1890s, whose owner, Horace Chase, also operated a hotel under the "Stags' Leap" name. The property fell into disrepair on Chase's death and the winery had long since ceased operations when it was purchased in the 1970s by Carl Doumani, who rebuilt it and began producing a rich Syrah wine under the Stags' Leap label.

After 1976, when his 1973 Cabernet Sauvignon had achieved world fame by outscoring the famous Bordeaux reds, Winiarski determined that the fame of his wine depended on the name—Stag's Leap. So he sued Carl Doumani for trademark infringement, claiming first use of the Stag's Leap name, and Doumani countersued, claiming that the use of the name in the 1870s by Horace Chase gave him first rights.[5] The case dragged on for almost a decade. Although everyone agreed that there was a likelihood of (and in fact there was) consumer confusion between the two identically-named wineries, the judge in the case was not able to find that either party had the right to use the name to the exclusion of the other. In a Solomonic decision, which the two men memorialized in an "apostrophic" settlement agreement, both wineries agreed to keep their names, but with the apostrophes in different places: Winiarski's Stag's Leap Wine Cellars had the right to put the apostrophe before the "s" and Doumani's Stags' Leap Winery had the right to put

Vignette (continued)

the apostrophe after the "s." After the settlement, the two men, who had been bitter enemies for almost 10 years, shook hands, took their families on a vacation together, and jointly released a 1985 Cabernet Sauvignon wine—a 50-50 blend from each winery—that they called "Accord."[6]

Shortly after this historic settlement, Napa wine growers pushed the federal government to adopt a Stags Leap District appellation, and Winiarski and Doumani found themselves this time on the same side opposing the proposal, which they argued would dilute both of their trademarks. They lost, and now the words "Stags Leap District" can appear on any wine made from grapes grown in the region where, according to legend, a mighty stag once saved himself from certain death.[7]

1. George M. Taber, Judgment of Paris: California vs. France and the Historic 1976 Paris Tasting that Revolutionized Wine 2 (Scribner 2005).

2. A list of the wines and rankings of the 1976 tasting is available at the Stag's Leap Wine Cellars official website, http://www.cask23.com/1976tasting.htm.

3. George Taber, the author of Judgment of Paris, was that Time magazine correspondent. See Judgment of Paris, Prologue, at 1-3.

4. Stag's Leap Wine Cellars official website: http://www.cask23.com/founders-vision.htm.

5. Frank J. Prial, Wine Talk, The New York Times, Feb. 9, 1994, http://query.nytimes.com/gst/fullpage.html?res=9EODEFDD1438F93AA.

6. Thom Elkjer, Lovable Rogue: Carl Doumani has an Uncanny Knack for Getting Into Just the Right Amount of Trouble, San Francisco Chronicle, Apr. 7, 2005, http://www.sfgate.com/cgi-bin/article.cgi?file=/c/a/2005/04/07/W1GOPC.

7. See Vignette: "Wine Labels—Appellation of Origin."

Imitation Is the Most Sincere Form of Flattery— Gallo Turns a New Leaf

Kendall-Jackson Winery, Ltd. v. E. & J. Gallo Winery, dba Turning Leaf Vineyards, 150 F.3d 1042 (9th Cir. 1998)

B y the late 1990s, the United States wine industry had changed dramatically. In earlier days the wine market had been dominated by low-budget bulk wine producers, with a few renowned wineries such as the Robert Mondavi Winery or Stag's Leap Wine Cellars producing high-end product at the other end of the spectrum. By the 1990s, the market had segmented into at least four levels: a low end, dominated by the bulk wines sold by the E. & J. Gallo Winery; a very high end, dominated by exclusive producers such as Harlan Estate, crafting selected varietals and priced accordingly; in a middle-high range, quality wines such as those produced at Stag's Leap Wine Cellars; and in a new middle-low range, cork-finished wines, with some aging, priced moderately at between $10 and $20 per bottle.[1]

---

1. Robert C. Eyler, *The International Competitiveness of the California Wine Industry*, Sonoma State University, Department of Economics, Rohnert Park, CA, http://www.libweb.sonoma.edu/regional/faculty/eyler/eyler.html.

In 1982, Jess Jackson, a San Francisco attorney, founded the Kendall-Jackson Winery, with a goal of producing quality wine at affordable prices.

These latter so-called "fighting varietals," led by Kendall-Jackson Winery, appealed to a wide range of newly minted wine buffs, had achieved market dominance in a short time, and had taken market share from the lower-priced generic jug wines for which the GALLO brand was famous. These moderately priced wines competed in a crowded category with not just domestic wines but also inexpensive imports from Argentina, Chile, and Australia, which had created a glut of wines in that price range in the market. Because of the proliferation of so many wines in such a short time, it became increasingly difficult for one producer to develop an original and distinctive brand that would catch consumers' eyes and enable them to distinguish one wine from another.

One of the more successful wineries to achieve brand recognition in this market was Kendall-Jackson Winery. Kendall-Jackson prided itself on the quality of its wines for the price and had spent widely in advancing its popular brand, "Vintner's Reserve," as a premium wine that was also affordable. Since the first vintages were put on the market in 1983, Kendall-Jackson's Vintner's Reserve wine had gained a significant market share in the fighting varietal category. By the 1990s, according to court filings, its Vintner's Reserve Chardonnay was the number one–selling Chardonnay wine in the United States. The labels for Kendall-Jackson's Vintner's Reserve wines were easily recognized, featuring a downward-pointing grape-leaf design in varied shades of green, orange, yellow, red, and brown. Across the leaf design ran a wide banner reading "KENDALL-JACKSON." Kendall-Jackson's Vintner's Reserve wine was sold in a recognizable bottle—either a Burgundy-style bottle (for the Chardonnay) or a Bordeaux-style bottle (for its Merlot), with a rounded flange and a visible cork with printed leaves on it, a brown or burgundy neck label with gold lines on the top and bottom, and an off-white label also featuring a multicolored leaf design.

The E. & J. Gallo Winery was at the time the largest wine producer in the world, but it had a reputation in the lower-priced wine category, as a maker of non-premium "jug" wine. As the court noted, while Kendall-Jackson was a leader in the mid-priced varietal wine market, the market for the lower-priced non-varietals had been declining. In 1992, Gallo had commenced market research to determine the best way to take advantage of changes in the wine industry and to enter the premium wine market. It then began the process for establishing its own premium winery, to be located at its vineyard properties in Sonoma County, in Northern California.[2] As part of this market research, according to facts brought out in the case, Gallo studied Kendall-Jackson's success. Through this research, Gallo began to understand that its trademark, "GALLO," was associated with inexpensive jug wine. It also learned that consumers associate a grape-leaf design on a wine bottle with a premium-quality wine.

In 1995, Gallo introduced a line of premium wines produced largely from its Sonoma County vineyards that did not use the Gallo name and that featured a grape-leaf design. It labeled this wine "Turning Leaf." The wines sold under this label were similar to Kendall-Jackson's Vintner's Reserve wines. They consisted

---

2. Id Robert C. Eyler, *The International Competitiveness of the California Wine Industry*, Sonoma State University, Department of Economics, Rohnert Park, CA, http://www.libweb.sonoma.edu/regional/faculty/eyler/eyler.html.

> *In 1977, the Gallo family began acquiring land in Sonoma County and began producing wines there in the early 1990s; Gallo of Sonoma was officially established in 1993, when its first wines were released.*

of varietals such as Chardonnay and Merlot, cork finished and priced less than $15 per bottle. They came in either a Burgundy-style or Bordeaux-style bottle and featured a rounded flange, a visible cork with printed leaves, a brown or burgundy neck label with gold lines on the top and bottom, and with a prominent downward-pointing leaf design in various shades of green, yellow, orange, red, and brown.

Even if it believed that imitation is the most sincere form of flattery, Kendall-Jackson did not feel honored. And it was not amused. Six months after Gallo introduced its "Turning Leaf" wines, Kendall-Jackson sued in federal district court for the Northern District of California for trademark infringement, trade dress infringement, trademark dilution, and trade dress dilution under the Lanham Act.[3] It also made unfair competition claims under California state law. The main thrust of its complaint was that Gallo had used a grape-leaf design and otherwise imitated Kendall-Jackson's trade dress for the purpose of deceiving consumers and "passing off" its wines for those that had been popularized by Kendall-Jackson. Kendall-Jackson also claimed that Gallo used wine bottles that mimicked the overall appearance of Kendall-Jackson's Vintner's Reserve bottles. The lower court dis-

---

3. 15 U.S.C. §§1125 et seq., *see*, Vignette: "Trademark Law in Brief."

agreed, however, and ruled against Kendall-Jackson on all counts. Kendall-Jackson appealed.

To prove its trademark infringement case, Kendall-Jackson had to demonstrate that its mark was distinctive and also that Gallo's use of the Turning Leaf mark created a likelihood of confusion. Therefore, the analysis turned on the same question as had been before the court in 1910, in the *Italian Swiss Colony* case:[4] was Kendall-Jackson's mark unique, and was it strong enough to merit protection? In other words, was the grape-leaf design on the Vintner's Reserve bottles so distinctive that a consumer would be unable to distinguish a bottle of Kendall-Jackson's Chardonnay from that produced by Gallo under the Turning Leaf label?

The district court had found that the grape-leaf design, separated from Kendall-Jackson's name printed on the banner across the front, was not sufficiently distinctive, because no consumer would associate a fall-colored leaf design as a symbol for Kendall-Jackson without the name of the winery on the banner. The appellate court agreed with this conclusion. The design, in its view, was merely suggestive of how wine is made: a grape leaf comes from a grapevine, which has grapes from which wine is produced. The court noted that "wine bottlers other than Kendall-Jackson have long used grape leaves to decorate their bottles." Thus, it ruled that grape-leaf designs had become generic symbols for wine and were not protectable as trademarks. Because the grape leaf is used widely in the industry, it no longer has the power to differentiate one brand of wine from another.

The court did note that a particular producer's grape leaf might be so distinctive as to warrant protection from copying. However, Kendall-Jackson's design was not that one. Its major

---

4. Italian Swiss Colony v. Italian Vineyard Company, 158 Cal. 252 (1910); *see* Case 1.

distinctive feature was the separation in the middle where the winery name was printed, and Gallo had not imitated that feature. Moreover, even though Gallo's leaf resembled Kendall-Jackson's, it was not exactly the same; its leaf folded and turned at an angle rather than pointing straight down.

Kendall-Jackson also lost on its trade dress claim. For this claim to be valid, Kendall-Jackson had to prove that the features on its wine bottles—the cork, flange, and neck label features—were non-functional and distinctive. This requirement is designed to ensure that trademark law, whose purpose is to protect a company's reputation and to prevent consumer confusion, is not used to enable a business to control a useful product feature in an anticompetitive manner. Unfortunately for Kendall-Jackson, the court found that, like its trademark, these features on its bottles were not distinctive. Moreover, in the court's view, Gallo had presented sufficient evidence to show that the combination of an exposed cork, rounded flange, and neck label create a "California look," which consumers now look for in a California wine. If the court were to allow Kendall-Jackson exclusive use of these features, the court worried, then other California wine producers would be at a competitive disadvantage. Further, this "California look" only tells consumers that the wine they are buying is from California. It would not tell them that the wine is produced by Kendall-Jackson.

Outside of its trademark claims, Kendall-Jackson also argued that Gallo's efforts to imitate its labels and the design of its bottles amounted to unfair competition. Gallo had conducted market studies before launching its "Turning Leaf" brand. Kendall-Jackson argued that Gallo had studied its success, identified the components of Kendall-Jackson's design that had contributed to that success, and then deliberately imitated exactly those features. And Kendall-Jackson claimed further that Gallo had gone so far as to negotiate with retailers the placement for its Turning Leaf wines next to Kendall-Jackson's Vintner's Reserve wines on the store shelf. All this, Kendall-Jackson argued, was for the purpose of taking advantage of, and profiting from, Kendall-Jackson's own substantial efforts at promoting its wines, and piggy-backing off its success. This behavior, the company concluded, was exactly what unfair competition laws were created to deter.

The court did not necessarily disagree with Kendall-Jackson on this argument. But this was an "equitable claim"—that is, Kendall-Jackson was asserting that Gallo had acted in a way that was not fair, and the person making an equitable claim has to have acted in a fair way itself. The court did not believe that Kendall-Jackson had been entirely candid when it gathered its evidence for its lawsuit against Gallo. In fact, Gallo had demonstrated that, just before bringing its case in 1996, Kendall-Jackson had apparently changed its own label for its Vintner's Reserve wines to make it more closely resemble the label that Gallo used on its Turning Leaf wines. Was the company trying to gain some benefit from Gallo's apparent success with these new wines, or was it trying to build a stronger case for itself, or was it some of both? Evidence also was produced that Kendall-Jackson may have used Gallo's trade secrets (its confidential marketing studies) obtained from a former Gallo director of marketing when gathering its evidence for the case.

As a postscript to this case, in 1999 Gallo took Kendall-Jackson to state court in California for malicious prosecution.[5] Gallo asserted that Kendall-Jackson had filed its trademark and unfair competition suit against Gallo for the sole and improper purpose of harassing Gallo and to prevent a new competitor from gaining

---

5. E. & J. Gallo Winery v. Kendall-Jackson Winery, Ltd., 76 Cal App. 4th 970 (5th Dist. 1999).

entry into the already crowded category of competitively priced varietal wines.

Kendall-Jackson defended against the suit using the ancient legal doctrine of "unclean hands." This doctrine was first propounded by the Courts in Equity in medieval England: a person bringing an action for equitable relief will be denied a remedy if he or she has acted unethically or in bad faith. Kendall-Jackson asserted that Gallo had engaged in improper behavior directed at Kendall-Jackson in the marketing of Turning Leaf wines. The state court agreed with this contention. Gallo representatives had used so-called "piggyback" adjacencies to put the lower-priced Gallo products next to Kendall-Jackson, the higher-priced category leader. Gallo employees allegedly had moved other branded wines from their place next to Kendall-Jackson products in stores and replaced them with Turning Leaf wines. If true, for an employee of a winery to move another winery's products in a store could have been a violation of both federal and state regulations. Kendall-Jackson also claimed that Gallo may have provided free labor to retailers in exchange for favorable product placement; in some locations, it accused Gallo employees of removing Kendall-Jackson wines entirely from their placement on shelves and of wearing retailer badges while stocking wines, even though they were not employed by the stores.

The court concluded that Gallo's marketing strategies targeting Kendall-Jackson's market share had contributed to Kendall-Jackson's decision to pursue an infringement action against Gallo. And even though Kendall-Jackson had not been able to prove its case in federal court, Gallo's own behavior, which the court judged to be unfair, would have justified Kendall-Jackson's motives for bringing the suit. Accordingly, in this action, the court could not find Kendall-Jackson's motives to be unjustified or malicious, and Gallo lost this round.

Vignette

Trademark Law in Brief

Trademark disputes in the wine industry are not
new, as the *Italian Swiss Colony* case described in
Case 1 illustrates. One of a modern winery's most
valuable assets is the name under which it sells its
wine, whether that is Mondavi, Stag's Leap, or Gallo.
If the winery sells its product into interstate or international
markets, that name may be protectable as a trademark under
federal law, the laws of the countries where the wine is sold, and
international treaties. Prior to the passage of the first trademark
laws in the United States (the Trademark Act of 1881, followed
by the Trademark Act of 1905), trademarks received common law
protection (that is, the law was handed down through precedents
in court decisions). Today, trademarks in the United States are
protected under the Lanham Act (the Trademark Act of 1946),
as amended.[1] Under the Lanham Act, a "trademark" is a word,
symbol, or device used to identify a producer's goods or services
sold. "Trade dress" is the entire selling image of a product,
including its packaging. The purpose of trademark law is to
prevent consumer confusion as to the source of the product,
and also to prevent unfair competition.

In the United States, the first user of any trademark is
protected from any subsequent use of a mark that looks like or
is confusingly similar to the protected mark in connection with
similar goods and services, or any likely area of expansion. To
be afforded federal protection under the Lanham Act, in addition
to whatever common law protections are available, a trademark
must be registered with the U.S. Patent and Trademark Office
and bear the symbol "®." Trademark rights are exclusive to the
holder of the mark, and the trademark cannot be used without
the consent of the holder under a license. A trademark license is
an agreement under which the trademark owner, the "licensor,"
allows another, the "licensee," to use the trademark for specific
products and usually in a specific geographic territory. To protect

Vignette (continued)

the goodwill of the licensor, the license generally includes provisions dealing with quality control and providing the licensor with monitoring rights. Trademark rights are afforded to the owner as long as the trademark is used in commerce. If the owner of a trademark does not use the mark for an extended period of time, fails to protest the unauthorized use of the mark by others, or lets others use the mark without adequate supervision, then federal law considers the mark abandoned.

Trademark infringement occurs when another violates the exclusive rights of the trademark holder in connection with similar goods or services where the violation is likely to cause consumer confusion. Consumer confusion occurs if the consumer believes that the products or services originated from the trademark owner. Where the respective marks or products or services are not identical, the focus of the assessment will be on the *likelihood* of confusion with respect to the actual or potential consumers of the trademark owner's goods or services, and not on whether the holders of the competing marks are actually competitors.

Trademark law offers greater protection to marks that are "strong"—that is, distinctive or unique. A weak mark, on the other hand, is one that is merely generic, such as a geographical place name, and this would not receive the same level of protection as a strong mark. Marks that are merely generic cannot be protected. Descriptive marks or marks based on a name can only be protected if they have become associated with a specific product manufacturer in the public's mind—that is, if they have acquired a secondary meaning.

A trademark becomes diluted when it ceases to signify a single source; its links to the owner of the mark have become blurred or diminished by unauthorized use. An example of how dilution works is the etymology of the word "zipper." This common noun is now used for any fastener with parallel rows of "teeth" that are interlocked by a sliding tab. However, "Zipper" was originally registered in 1925 as a B.F. Goodrich trademark for overshoes with fasteners and at the time was a unique word. Unfortunately for Goodrich, very quickly the name became popularly used to refer to any fastener, not just for boots, and therefore lost its uniqueness and its trademark protection for most uses. Goodrich sued in an effort to protect its trademark, but federal trademark law at the time did not afford owners the ability to prevent uses which, even though not directly competitive, would dilute a mark. This was changed under amendments to the Lanham Act in 1996. Under these amendments, the owner of a famous mark can stop another person's commercial use of a mark or trade name if such use begins after the mark has become famous and causes dilution of the distinctive quality of the mark. There is no specific definition of "famous," but it relates to factors such as how distinctive the mark is or has become, how long it has been used in connection with the goods or services with which it is used, how much advertising and publicity surrounds the mark, how widely the mark is used, to what degree the mark is recognized, and how similar is it to other marks.[2]

---

1. 5 U.S.C. §§ 1125 *et seq.*
2. 15 U.S.C.A. § 1125(c).

The Changing Napa Valley— A Sleepy Outpost Becomes an International Destination

Scruby v. Vintage Grapevine, Inc.,
37 Cal. App. 4th 697 (1st Dist. 1995)

At the same time as the Napa Valley became a center for fine-wine production in the 1980s and 1990s, and an incredibly popular destination for tourists to the San Francisco Bay Area, it also was attracting new residents from the Bay Area who were seeking sites for second or retirement homes. This has caused significant congestion along the State Highway 29 corridor (St. Helena Highway), the main artery between towns in the lower valley, such as Napa and Yountville, and those farther north, such as St. Helena and Calistoga. For along this road is located some of the most prime vineyard and winery real estate in the entire valley, including several of the older, well-established wineries, such as the Charles Krug Winery and the Robert Mondavi Winery, as well as newer wineries established at the end of the twentieth century, including Cosentino Winery, which

claims to be the first stop on the highway as you enter Yountville.[1] The onslaught of tourists has provoked controversy and disputes among the affected parties: new homeowners from the Bay Area seeking to enhance and maintain their property values; old-time residents nostalgic for the days when the valley was a sleepy community; and wineries and vineyards, which need the road and access to it to conduct their agricultural business.

John and Giovanna Scruby had acquired an acre of land in Yountville along Highway 29 before the most recent onslaught of development. They built a single-family residence on their parcel. In 1990, Vintage Grapevine, Inc. acquired the lots next door to the Scruby home, comprising approximately 3.5 acres, on which they constructed the Cosentino Winery and planted vineyards. The Scrubys' property was landlocked, and access was provided by means of an easement over the winery's property to Highway 29. This easement was non-exclusive, 52 feet in width, for road and utility purposes. The easement initially had been created in the 1960s in connection with a planned residential subdivision that never was completed. This easement remained in place when the Scrubys acquired their land and built their home, and was unchanged when Grapevine later acquired the remaining land. Be-

---

1. Cosentino Winery official website, http://www.cosentinowinery.com/cosentino/page/tasting-rooms.jsp.

cause the property had not been subdivided, the easement area was far larger than necessary for access to a single parcel, and most of the easement area had never been used as a road.

From the time the winery first opened its doors, a conflict brewed between the two property owners. In connection with its winery and vineyard operations, Grapevine had located some water tanks and had planted grapevines inside the 52-foot easement area that the Scrubys had been using to access their property. A paved road was built, but it was shared among the Scrubys and their visitors, the winery operators, and the visitors to the winery's tasting room. The Scrubys objected to this increased activity on their road and complained that vehicles coming to and leaving the winery tasting room parking lot impeded their access. Eventually they took matters into their own hands and paved over another part of the 52-foot easement area on Grapevine's land just a few feet from the winery's driveway, and installed a new road to provide direct access to their residence from Highway 29. This new road did not meet design criteria approved by Napa County and the California State Department of Transportation (CDOT), which had been imposed because of traffic congestion along the Highway 29 corridor. Both agencies had insisted when Grapevine's winery was approved that having a single access at that location was critical to ensure the public safety. Accordingly, because the Scrubys' new road was located across Grapevine's land, the county threatened to revoke Grapevine's use permit for the operation of the winery.

In 1993 the Scrubys sued Grapevine, seeking to force the winery to remove its grapevines and water tanks from their easement area. They also wanted the winery to correct a drainage problem that created ponding on their side of the common road. Grapevine cross-complained against the Scrubys, asking the court to keep the Scrubys from interfering with its use of the property and to order the Scrubys to remove their new road and to restore Grapevine's property.

The trial court ruled against the Scrubys and they appealed.

The question before the appellate court was what rights the Scrubys held under the easement. They argued that the easement area could only be used for access, even though it was much wider than necessary for such purpose. They also maintained that the correct interpretation of the easement language would allow them the exclusive use of the *entire* easement area, which meant the right to use every inch of their 52-foot-wide easement for road purposes and for nothing else. Moreover, under this interpretation, Grapevine would be obliged to ensure unimpeded access at all times (even if this meant limiting the use of its own vehicles in the easement area and the number of tourist vehicles coming into the tasting room parking). The court disagreed.

"An easement is a restricted right to specific, limited, definable use or activity upon another's property, which right must be *less* than the right of ownership," the court ruled. In other words, the Scrubys did not own the land where the easement was located, just the right to pass over the land to access their own property. The court noted that the owner of an easement had to take care to use his or her rights "in such a way as to impose *as slight a burden as possible*" [emphasis added] on the property of the person granting the easement." Thus, the court concluded that the extent of the Scrubys' right to use Grapevine's land was limited—only to come and go over the land to and from their own property in as unobtrusive a manner as possible.

The Scrubys had maintained that Grapevine had encroached on their free access by using it for agricultural equipment, the planting of grapevines, and other winery-related activities that involved more than access. Before the winery had been located there, the easement area had been unimpeded, and the Scrubys wanted it to remain so. But the court pointed out that the Scrubys' use was *non-exclusive*. In other words, the idea of encroachment would be meaningful only if the entire easement area had been granted to the Scrubys for their sole and exclusive use. But that was not the case. They held their rights in conjunction with others and, accordingly, had to share. And as long as Grapevine did not unreasonably interfere with the Scrubys' access, it could do what it pleased with its property.

On the other hand, by installing their own road across the easement area, the Scrubys had both damaged Grapevine's property (by ripping out valuable grapevines) and had put Grapevine's use permit at risk. The court noted that although the Scrubys had the right to do what was reasonably necessary to repair and maintain the existing road to ensure their own access, they did not have the right to substantially alter the area, including relocating the road or installing an entirely new road, which they had done, without Grapevine's consent.

Due to the safety concerns expressed by the DOT and adjoining owners when the permit for the Cosentino Winery was issued, Napa County had expressly conditioned its approvals to require a single entrance to and from Highway 29 onto Grapevine's property for both the Scrubys' and the winery's use. The Scrubys had been given an opportunity to object to this arrangement at the public hearings, but apparently had not done so. Whether or not they had opposed it, once the use permit was in place, they could not unilaterally take measures, such as creating a second opening onto Highway 29, that would be in violation of that permit, thus putting the winery's continued operation in jeopardy. They were ordered to remove the new paved road and to restore the Grapevine property at their expense.

It is easy to understand how a conflict like this can arise. The Napa Valley had been a relatively calm place to live before the onslaught of tourism to the area. At the time the easement was created in 1966, the land that would eventually be sold to Grapevine was vacant and no longer in use for agricultural purposes. When the Scrubys bought their land, Highway 29 was busier, but there had been relatively little development in the Yountville area where the property was located. The more popular wineries that drew weekend visitors, such as the Robert Mondavi Winery or the Louis Martini Winery, were located farther north, nearer to Oakville and St. Helena. One can imagine that the Scrubys had lived quietly for many years before Grapevine bought the adjoining land and completely transformed their bucolic neighborhood. By the 1990s, however, the popularity of the entire valley had pushed winery development south and had completely overwhelmed Highway 29 (as the only true artery through the valley from north to south), especially in the summer and fall, and on weekends throughout the year, creating constant congestion, with cars entering and leaving winery tasting room parking lots. Traffic was even more dangerous in the late afternoon, when drivers who had tasted more than one glass of wine were less inhibited and willing to take more chances. When the permits for the Cosentino Winery were issued, one can imagine that the Scrubys could not have foretold the impact of sharing a road with a winery tasting room until they had actually experienced it.[2] It is easy to imagine their sense of frustration and loss to find themselves now living, essentially, in the middle of a winery tasting area. But they had to follow the rules laid out by the county, and choosing to build their own road may have seemed like an easy enough solution to their problem, but it turned out to be a very bad and costly idea.

---

2. According to the Cosentino Winery's website, it is open seven days per week, from 10:00 a.m. until 5:00 p.m. http://www.cosentinowinery.com/cosentino/page/tasting-rooms.jsp.

Vignette

What is "*Terroir*"?
What Is an Appellation?
Why Napa?

A wine drinker can go to a shop in New York City or Philadelphia or Miami and purchase a bottle of wine from California's Napa Valley. But the experience of tasting it after purchase does not match up to the magic, the vibrancy of tasting the same wine in the region, in the cellar, where the wine was made. This by itself explains why so many tourists to California make the drive up to the Napa Valley, to join the procession of other wine tasters along Highway 29, the St. Helena Highway, although the beauty of the place itself, the hills on either side of the road, the frequent light fog that tops those hills, creating a soft and delicate light, all spell romance and mystery, to enhance the ambience. Then there is the association of the wine with its own place, the scent of the cellar, dark and earthy, and the enthusiasm of those pouring the wine. This, in a nutshell, gives body to the total experience of "*terroir*" in a good wine.

What is *terroir*? Loosely defined, it is French for "soil." But it is so much more than that. It is not just the character of the soil (chalky, gravelly, sandy) in which the vines are planted, but rather the totality of factors that tell the taster that the wine was produced in that place from grapes that were grown there. It includes the altitude of the vineyard, for example, and its position relative to the sun—wines made from the same varietal grown on the east-facing side of the hills of the Napa Valley are reputed to be different from those grown on the west-facing hills. Sometimes wine producers in the United States substitute the term "microclimate" for *terroir* to describe the various areas within the Napa Valley. This probably derives also from the French word "*climat*," which in the Burgundy region of France is more commonly used than *terroir* to account for the many distinguishing factors in a vineyard area, such as

101

Vignette (continued)

soil, drainage, the bearing of the sun, and the slope of the
vineyard. Burgundians are amused that California winemakers
from time to time have taken cuttings of Pinot Noir grapevines
from vineyards in Burgundy, smuggled them into California, and
planted them in the Napa Valley and other regions in an effort to
create a vineyard that would produce a wine capable of standing
up to those wines produced from the ancient vineyards of the
Côte d'Or in eastern France. They know that the *"climat"* of
Northern California is not that of Burgundy, and that the wine
produced might be very good, but it would never be a true
wine of the Burgundy region. For those who understand wine
and its production know that very different wines can result from
neighboring vineyards—or even plots within the same vineyard.

In the United States, instead of using *"terroir"* and *"climat,"* wine specialists commonly refer to "microclimates." This word encompasses those various factors that result in the complexity of a good wine. In California, the consideration of microclimate has evolved into a system of classification that accounts for the variety of temperatures at which grapes may be grown within the state and even within the Napa Valley. There are five established climate regions in California. The coolest (Climate Region I) is similar to the Champagne or Côte d'Or regions of France and can be found as far south as the Santa Cruz mountains and as far north as Mendocino County, but also includes areas of Napa. Pinot Noir grapes grow well in this climate region. Climate Region II is similar to France's Bordeaux region and also is found in parts of Napa. Cabernet Sauvignon, Chardonnay, and Merlot grapes grow well in these areas. Climate Region III is warmer, equivalent to France's Rhone region, and also includes parts of Napa. The Carignan grape grows well here. Climate Region IV is similar to Southern Spain and includes regions south of the Napa Valley, including Sacramento and Yolo counties. And the hottest region, Climate Region V, which is similar to North Africa, is far to the South of the Napa Valley, in the San Joaquin Valley. It stands to reason, then, that a wine blended from grapes grown in the much hotter San Joaquin Valley or the Lodi region would be different in character from a wine made entirely from grapes grown in the Napa Valley. According to testimony that was presented in the *Bronco Wine Company* case,[1] the Napa Valley is an area where unique conditions exist to create wines of exceptional quality of various varieties, because of the presence of so many microclimates within one relatively small area. Globally, few regions have comparable growing conditions, and that makes the Napa Valley a very special place that people want to experience firsthand.[2] Hence the traffic congestion on Highway 29. It is unlikely that this corridor will ever be the bucolic country road that it was only 30 years ago.

---

1. Bronco Wine Company v. Jolly, 129 Cal. App. 4th 989 (3rd Dist. 2005), Case 11.
2. Bronco Wine Co. v. Jolly, 129 Cal. App. 4th 989 (3d Dist. 2005), at n.12.

You Can't Take It with You, or Have It Shipped Either—

Direct Shipment: The Supreme Court Weighs In

Granholm v. Heald, 544 U.S. 460 (2005)

As the wine industry, particularly in California, has expanded in the last 25 years, the tasting rooms of Napa and Sonoma County wineries have become popular tourist venues. These are attractions in themselves, not just places to taste wine but often art galleries, historical sites, and, of course, gift shops where a wide variety of wine-themed souvenirs can be purchased.

Any visitor to the San Francisco Bay area making a pilgrimage to the Napa Valley can acquire a set of wine glasses, perhaps some olive oil soaps or bottles of olive oil, and have them shipped back to her home in, say, Austin or Baltimore without any question. So she should be able to have a case of the winery's Cabernet Sauvignon shipped directly to her home also, right? Maybe not. It would depend on where she lives. The winery could ship the wine to Austin as long as it kept within certain vol-

ume limits. But if this unfortunate tourist lives in Baltimore, then she is probably out of luck. In the state of Maryland, direct shipments of wine to an individual are prohibited.

So if you fall in love with a luscious Pinot Noir or fruity Chardonnay during a visit to the Napa Valley, you risk a felony charge if you live in Baltimore and try to have it shipped to your home. You have to jump through a number of hoops, including designating a Maryland-licensed wholesaler to receive the wine shipment and purchasing it (with an appropriate markup, of course) through a licensed distributor in the state. Even the well-known wine critic, Robert Parker, who lives and works out of his home in Monkton, Maryland, was for a long while not able to have wine sent directly to him to evaluate in *The Wine Advocate* newsletter that he publishes until he obtained a permit from the state liquor board.[1]

This type of law, which is not unique to Maryland, has effectively created a monopoly for domestic wine sellers and limited choices for consumers in those states that restrict direct shipment. Thus, wine bloggers generated enormous enthusiasm in early 2005 in anticipation of the Supreme Court decision in *Granholm v. Heald*. The case was a consolidation of three challenges to direct-shipment prohibitions in Michigan and New York state. The appellate courts in two different circuits had reached opposite conclusions regarding the enforceability of these laws. In the two Michigan cases, the Sixth Circuit Court of Appeals had struck down that state's prohibition,[2] while the Second Circuit had upheld the New York state requirements.[3] Wine enthusiasts optimistically predicted that the Supreme Court would take this opportunity to throw out the "crazy quilt" of state restrictions on direct shipment and "open the cellar door" to wineries to ship their product freely throughout the country.

Alas, they were too hopeful and not good judges of how courts—and particularly the Supreme Court—function. It was wildly optimistic to imagine that the Court would throw out an entire body of prior law and completely disregard the judgment of numerous state legislatures, simply to allow some wine buffs to shop more freely and taste more widely. For these enthusiasts, then, the Court's decision in the *Granholm* case was a disappointment. In a 5-4 opinion delivered by Justice Anthony Kennedy, the Court struck down the requirements of both states, but the relief the Court afforded was not what the direct ship-

---

1. ECHIKSON, NOBLE ROT 104.
2. Heald v. Engler, 342 F. 3d 517 (6th Cir. 2003).
3. Swedenburg v. Kelly, 358 F. 3d 223 (2d Cir. 2004).

ment advocates had wished. Ultimately, however, although the final decision was less than momentous, it nevertheless threw a number of state restrictions—some of which had been in place since the repeal of Prohibition, and not just in Michigan and New York, but in more than half the states in the continental United States—into question.

Today many Americans regard alcoholic beverages, and especially beer and wine, as ordinary consumer items, no different from olive oil or soap. But, as Justice Stevens pointed out in his dissenting opinion in *Granholm*, this was not the case in 1919, when the Eighteenth Amendment prohibiting the sale of alcoholic beverages nationally was ratified, or in 1933, when Prohibition was repealed by the Twenty-first Amendment. Once the federal government backed away from prohibiting the sale and use of alcoholic beverages, states stepped in to fill the void, putting in place laws that reflected the then majority viewpoint in the United States: that alcoholic beverages, including wine, were inherently dangerous, requiring extensive regulation and control to protect the states' residents from their deleterious effects. And before the rise in popularity of wine and wine tourism in the United States, the restrictions set out in most states' alcoholic beverage regulations, although annoying to a few, did not appear to be particularly onerous. No groundswell occurred to change them until the last two decades of the twentieth century, during which time annual wine consumption in the United States doubled, with an increased interest in fine wine and a rapid expansion in the number of small boutique wineries in states as disparate as New York and Virginia. Many of these smaller wineries—so-called *"garagistes"* (after boutique winemakers in the Bordeaux wine region of France who literally used the garages attached to their homes as wine cellars)—produced only a few thousand cases per year, and their wines could not be found in local wine shops, because they were too small to access the large distribution networks in any given state. But they could be found online.

At the same time, consumers (who by then were not only accustomed to having purchases made in stores and by catalogue sent to them by mail but also had become avid Internet shoppers) were eager to taste these lesser-known wines and to have them shipped directly to their homes. The fact that information about so many wines was prevalent on winery Web sites and also through wine newsletters and Internet blogs added to the frustration of these consumers, who were tantalized by descriptions of luscious wines only to learn that they had no practical way to obtain them because of what they viewed as arcane regulations preventing direct shipping that seemed to be from a far different era. And it seemed that the more restrictive laws were in states such as New York, Florida, Maryland, and Virginia—states that, after California, had the country's largest number of wine consumers, sophisticated enthusiasts eager to try new offerings from small out-of-state wineries.

At the time the Supreme Court agreed to consider the issue of direct wine shipment, state wine distribution regulation generally followed one of two patterns. Either every drop of wine had to pass through the three-tier system, from producer to distributor to retailer, or the state allowed in-state wineries to sell directly to consumers, but prohibited such sales to out-of-state wineries. This was the case in both Michigan and New York. The motive of the states in this latter example was to promote the growth of the nascent wine industry within the state. Wine distributors, for their part, largely opposed allowing direct shipment by anyone, seeing even this small-scale practice as a threat to their industry, and claiming that they formed a bulwark against criminal influences in the liquor industry and illegal sales of liquor to minors over the Internet. On the other hand, wine consumers and the out-of-state wineries that were prohibited from shipping directly to them argued that these prohibitions in favor of in-state wineries were discriminatory and a violation of the Commerce Clause.[4]

In *Granholm,* the Court assessed the regulatory scheme in the two states. The plaintiff in the Michigan case, Domaine Alfred, was a small winery located in San Luis Obispo, California. It produced 3,000 cases of wine per year. It had received requests for its wine from Michigan consumers but could not fill orders because of the state's direct-shipment ban. Most alcoholic beverages in Michigan were distributed through the state's three-tier system. Wineries, whether located in-state or out-of-state, generally sold only to licensed in-state retailers. Licensed retailers sold to consumers, through stores and, in limited circumstances, through home delivery. However, an exception was made for Michigan's approximately 40 in-state wineries that could obtain a "winemaker" license, allowing them to ship directly to in-state consumers. Out-of-state wineries could apply for an "outside seller of wine" license, but this only allowed them to sell to in-state wholesalers. According to briefs filed with the Court, even if the Domaine Alfred winery could have found a Michigan distributor to sell its wine, the wholesaler's markup would have made the sale economically infeasible. The only cost-effective way for it to sell its wine other than locally was over the Internet, and it was prevented from doing so by Michigan's laws. On the other hand, Michigan wineries could legally sell wine directly to Michigan residents through online sales.

In the New York case, Juanita Swedenburg and David Lucas were the plaintiffs. Swedenburg owned a small winery in Virginia (the Swedenburg Estate Vineyard) and Lucas a small California

---

4. U.S. CONST., Art. I, Section 8.

winery (The Lucas Winery). Some of their customers were tourists from other states who purchased their wine during tastings at the wineries. But customers residing in New York state could not order Swedenburg or Lucas wines to be shipped directly to their homes. To ship directly to New York consumers, the wineries would have been required to open a branch office, a storeroom, or a warehouse within the state of New York, something that would have been prohibitively expensive for a small winery. In fact, it was so prohibitive that, according to Justice Kennedy in the majority opinion in *Granholm*, not a single out-of-state winery had availed itself of New York's direct-shipping privilege.

After considering the history of wine regulation both pre- and post-Prohibition, and the briefs submitted by the parties and all the interested trade groups, the *Granholm* majority concluded that both the Michigan and New York schemes granted in-state wineries access to the state's consumers on preferential terms. As the Court noted, in the absence of federal legislation, the "negative" or so-called "dormant" Commerce Clause prohibits a state from passing laws affecting interstate commerce, particularly laws favoring an in-state business over out-of-state businesses. Therefore, all things being equal, the New York and Michigan regulatory schemes violated the Commerce Clause.

But the analysis did not end there, because what was at stake was not olive oil or soap, but wine. Thus, the issue was complicated by Section 2 of the Twenty-first Amendment to the Constitution. This provision was enacted at the time of repeal of Prohibition to allow states broad authority to regulate the sale of alcoholic beverages within their borders. It reads:

> The transportation or importation into any State, Territory, or possession of the United States for delivery or use therein of intoxicating liquors in violation of the laws thereof, is hereby prohibited.

Those arguing in favor of Michigan's and New York's regulations maintained that this clause broadly allows states to treat those importing alcohol into the state in any manner they see fit, if such regulation has a legitimate purpose of protecting the state's residents. This could, if necessary, result in permissible discrimination against out-of-state wineries. The states further argued that prior to Prohibition, the wine industry was made up of small local wineries in almost every community, and that large so-called "corporate" wineries, which took root particularly in California, only developed as a result of Prohibition. California wineries did not suffer so much from Prohibition, they continued, and therefore were able to recover more quickly and to take advantage of the failures of the local wine industries. It was therefore rational for a state to put in place a system more protective of small, nascent local wineries, because the California wine industry had a 50-year advantage over these local producers.

The Court in *Granholm* rejected these arguments, concluding that none of them justified treating out-of-state producers differently from in-state vintners. According to the Court, this was a privilege that states did not have pre-Prohibition, and they did not receive authority to pass discriminatory laws in the Twenty-first Amendment. Such discrimination was therefore unconstitutional. The Court concluded that states were free to regulate the direct shipment of wine as they saw fit, as long as they treated in-state and out-of-state wineries equally and uniformly. In other words, the Court did not question the constitutionality of an absolute three-tier system of regulation. And it did not mandate any particular direction for states to take. A state may ban or allow direct shipments of wine as long as the decision applies equally to all wineries.

So, what is the practical impact of *Granholm* on our wine buff from Baltimore? Practically none. She is still not able to have wine shipped directly to her home. The actual ruling did not automatically change any laws or legalize direct shipping. Legislation that would open up direct shipment in Maryland was introduced in the state legislature in March 2008, but unless and until it passes, Maryland law will remain as it existed before the *Granholm* decision. And in other states, the result has been mixed. In May 2005, at the time *Granholm* was decided, 26 states allowed direct shipping of wine to consumers. By 2007, 34 states allowed some form of direct shipping, but frequently with some hurdles.

And for at least one of the plaintiffs in *Granholm*, the Swedenburg Estate Vineyard, the "victory" was pyrrhic at best. Although New York state was not permitted to discriminate against Juanita Swedenburg, she ultimately lost in her home state of Virginia. Before *Granholm*, Virginia wineries were free to ship directly to shops and restaurants. After *Granholm*, a 2005 Virginia court decision prohibited such sales, with the result that small wineries, such as Swedenburg Estate, that used to get their wines directly into restaurants faced the prospect of seeing their sales revenues decrease due to wholesaler markups.[5]

And the battle is far from over. The Court in *Granholm* put the burden on the states to show a legitimate purpose that would justify apparent discrimination. A number of states have made a few changes to their direct shipment laws in an effort to comply with *Granholm*, such as allowing direct shipping for both instate and out-of-state wineries up to a relatively low volume limit, or permitting direct shipment only to consumers who purchase the wine in person at the winery. The state of Massachusetts modified its regulations to allow direct shipping only by

---

5. Juanita Swedenburg died in the summer of 2007; she was 82 years old. It is now up to her children to carry on the battle to open up Virginia's direct-shipping laws.

wineries that produce less than 30,000 gallons of wine each year. Coincidentally, none of the wineries in Massachusetts produced over 30,000 gallons at the time the legislation was enacted, so effectively all Massachusetts wineries were allowed to direct-ship to consumers, although many larger but still small out-of-state wineries continued to be prohibited from doing so. These various efforts have, of course, brought further legal challenges. For example, a group of smaller California wineries has sued the state of Massachusetts under *Granholm*, arguing that the degree of discrimination is irrelevant in analyzing whether a state law violates the Commerce Clause.[6] And consumers are as confused as ever, if not more so, because they believe that an important Supreme Court decision that grabbed headlines in 2005 must have changed something.

The result of this confusion is a continuation of technically illegal wine shipments. Just as in Prohibition, when the law was frequently ignored, consumers who are determined to get a certain wine will persist in finding the means, no matter where they live. It is well known, for example, that residents of the state of Arkansas, which has some of the more restrictive rules in the nation, including several "dry" counties where no alcohol can be sold, procure wine simply by driving over the state borders and bringing it back in the trunks of their cars. Other resolute consumers travel to California and carry the wine back in their luggage, risking disappointing breakage and spoiled clothing. In February 2008, the Wines and Spirits Wholesalers of America (WSWA), the trade association of wine wholesalers, voiced "grave concern" about the widespread practice of shipping wine across state lines to consumers in a letter sent to liquor control

---

6. Family Winemakers of California v. Jenkins, No. 1:06-CV-11682 (D. Mass.) Sept. 18, 2007.

boards and attorneys general in all 50 states. According to the WSWA, "illegal alcohol trafficking" is rampant in the wine industry and attention must be paid.[7] It most likely will. The goal of the direct-shipment lobby is to open up all 50 states to direct shipping; the goal of the distributors' lobbies is to retain the three-tier system that has been the basis of their industry for more than 70 years. The battle is definitely not over.

---

7. News Release, Wines and Spirits Wholesalers of America, Feb. 26, 2008, *available at* http://www.wswa.org/public/media/20080226.html.

The Three-Tier Distribution System

State Regulation of Wine and Wineries

Throughout its history as a colony and a nation, the United States and the individual states have tried through various means to regulate the sale and use of alcoholic beverages. In fact, nothing else used in American society, not even weapons, has faced such varied, complicated, and persistent regulation as alcohol: its production, its containers, its labeling, and its pricing, who can sell it, how and where it is to be sold and drunk, and whether it can be sold at all, and who is allowed to purchase and drink it. National Prohibition through the Eighteenth Amendment represented the most extreme form of alcoholic beverage regulation. But if anything, its impact on drinking patterns in the United States was no stronger than during the period after Repeal in 1933, as a new web of regulations was woven by the various states. A few states retained Prohibition. In fact, the last of these, Mississippi, did not repeal its "dry" laws until 1966, and in some states, such as Arkansas, dry counties remain to this day.[1]

Most states, however, either created state monopolies to handle all liquor sales, including wine and beer, or formed state agencies to issue licenses for the production, distribution, and sale of alcoholic beverages. This latter system is known as the "three-tier" system. These state liquor control boards have exercised a broad range of control over the ways and means by which alcohol is made, advertised, sold, and consumed.

The result has been chaotic, to say the least. Taxes vary widely, leading to a wide range of prices for the same bottle of wine depending on in which state it is sold. In some states, one can purchase wine in a private store, even if "distilled" liquor (including, by state definition, non-distilled beverages such as sweet or fortified wines with a high alcohol content) can only be purchased in a state-controlled store. Sometimes wine can be purchased in drug stores, but not in grocery stores. This confusion created by a balkanized regulatory scheme illustrates two obvious facts: first, in the United States, attitudes about wine and its sale still carry the legacy of Prohibition almost a century after its enactment, and second, wine cannot be viewed or treated as a simple commodity like cheese or chocolate.

A three-tier system consists of the following levels: manufacturer, distributor, and retailer. Manufacturers sell product to the distributors who, in turn, sell the product to the retailer. Each carries a separate license from the state, and a licensee in one tier, such as a winemaker, cannot also be licensed in the state in another of the tiers. Thus a winery cannot also establish retail wine shops separate from the winery, and a distributor cannot obtain a license to make wine. The reason behind this restriction was the perceived social ill of brewers operating their own bars or saloons (which had been one of the primary justifications for Prohibition in the first place). The fear of a proliferation of saloons after Repeal caused states to look for ways to keep alcohol producers away from alcohol sellers.

Over time, modifications to the three-tier system have been adopted in a number of states. For example, many states allow wineries to self-distribute to retailers and restaurants, although often these privileges have been extended only to small, start-up wineries making a limited number of cases of wine per year (for example, 1,000 cases or less). Some allow direct shipment to restaurants and retail shops in the state but not to consumers' homes. Others allow direct shipment to consumers, but not to restaurants or retail establishments.

With the loosening of regulation, ironically, have come the legal challenges to aspects of the three-tier system, such as discrimination in favor of in-state wineries over out-of-state producers (*Granholm*) and challenges to pricing regulations (*Costco*).[2] The three-tier system over time has allotted significant power to the wine distribution industry. States depend on distributors to collect the lucrative excise taxes paid on wine

Vignette (continued)

sales each year. Distributors also play an unofficial enforcement role—refusing to supply retailers who have had legal problems or who have a history of selling to minors. They also notify states of violations of direct-shipping restrictions and other regulations. Wine distributors argue that they play a critical role in protecting the state and its residents by ensuring the collection of taxes, by preventing the sale of alcohol to minors, and by limiting the consumption of alcoholic beverages in general.[3]

Whether a winery can get into the right distribution networks within a particular state or not can determine its success or failure. As the distribution industry has consolidated over the past two decades, locating a distributor and getting a favorable contract has become almost impossible in some states for small start-up wineries. This has led to criticism of the three-tier system and of the role played by wholesalers: that it limits diversity in wine selection and increases costs for all. A typical wholesaler markup can be 25 percent, which adds a lot to the price ultimately paid by the consumer.

---

1. David J. Hanson, "Dry Counties," *Alcohol: Problems and Solutions*, http://www2.potsdam.edu/hansondj/controversies/1140551076.html.

2. Costco Wholesale Corporation v. Hoen, No. 06-35543, Jan. 29, 2008, ___ F. 3d ___ (9th Cir. 2008); *See* Case 10.

3. *See*, Costco Wholesale Corporation v. Hoen, Nos. 06-35538, 06-35542, and 06-35543, Brief of the National Beer Wholesalers Association and Wine and Spirits Wholesalers of America, Inc., as *Amicus Curiae* in support of Defendants-Appellants, filed Nov. 10, 2006.

We Can't Get It for You Wholesale— Costco Takes On the Three-Tier System

Costco Wholesale Corp. v. Hoen, No. 06-35543, Jan. 29, 2008, ___ F.3d ___ (9th Cir. 2008)

Saturday afternoon at any Costco Wholesale store in the United States: entire families pushing giant-sized shopping carts through a crowded warehouse facility stacked almost to the ceiling with pallets and racks of very large packages of every type of consumer item anyone would want to buy. Aisles are filled with jars of pickles, boxes of plastic bags, clothing, furniture, audio equipment, wide-screen televisions, computers, pharmaceuticals, makeup, flowers, meat, fresh vegetables, frozen foods, auto care products, jewelry, and beverages, including wine (in those states where wine is permitted to be sold in grocery stores). All of these products are offered at a significant reduction over customary retail prices. How does Costco do it?

Costco Wholesale Corporation is a Washington state–based national chain of membership discount buying clubs with millions of members in the United States and Canada. Costco's success is based on the concept of offering its members low prices on a limited selection of products within a very wide range of merchandise categories. Rapid inventory turnover in its stores and high sales numbers result from operating efficiencies and volume purchasing, efficient distribution, and self-service product selection in the stores. It buys in bulk directly from the producers most of the products it sells, eliminating the middleman and an entire distribution chain. This results in significant cost savings that Costco is able to pass on to its members. In most cases, this business model works. But for wine, it has been a different story in three-tier states—one that independent distributors have not wanted to change.

For decades after the institution of the three-tier system, in most states, distributors enjoyed a virtual monopoly in the sale and distribution of alcoholic beverages. But amendments to the laws, for example, to allow wineries to sell directly to consumers, have eroded the distributors' hold on the market. Therefore, the distribution industry evidenced strong concern when, in 2004, Costco sued the state of Washington in an effort to overthrow its three-tier system, viewing this challenge as a significant threat to its bottom line. With the growth of the big-box retail industry, the large chains and warehouse stores, such as Costco, represent a lucrative market for distributors. Costco claims to be one of the largest wine retailers in the United States. A distributor's profit margin is greater when it can deliver, say, 2,000 cases of wine in one shipment to a big-box store like Costco than to make many deliveries of only a few cases to a number of small retail shops.

But Costco's business model does not, as a general rule, rely on distributors. By receiving shipments of wine directly from wineries in California, for example, Costco is able to offer a variety of good wines at low cost. But in Costco's home state, Washington, it was unable to take full advantage of this business model when it came to buying wine for sale in its stores there, because Washington's Liquor Control Board (LCB) imposed certain requirements on distributors and retailers that resulted in higher uniform prices on wines sold in that state. At the time of its lawsuit in 2004, Costco claimed that it was paying 4 percent more on average for Washington-state-made wine in Washington than it was for the same wine when shipped to its stores in California.[1]

The Washington state law imposed a number of restrictive requirements: it required both distributors and retailers to mark up prices at least 10 percent; it outlawed volume discounts; it prohibited retailers from buying beer or wine on credit and prevented them from storing wine or beer at their central warehouse; and it required wholesalers to post wine and beer prices with the state LCB and to hold them in place for 30 days (post-and-hold requirement).[2] Costco argued in its suit that these restrictions violated the Sherman Antitrust Act because they were anticompetitive, and the district court ruled in Costco's favor.[3] The court ruled that Washington's posting, holding, minimum markup, delivered pricing, uniform pricing, ban on volume discounts, and ban on credit sale requirements conflicted with federal antitrust laws. The Ninth Circuit Court of Appeals overturned the district court's ruling on most counts, upholding most

---

1. Plaintiff's Expert Report of Keith Leffler, Associate Professor of Economics, University of Washington, June 3, 2005.

2. RCW 66.28.185, RCW 66.28.070, and implementing regulations, Washington Administrative Code (WAC) 314-20-100(2), (5); WAC 314-24-190 (2), (5).

3. Costco also argued that the state laws violated the Commerce Clause of the U.S. Constitution because they discriminated against out-of-state wineries. The court ruled in favor of Costco on this argument on the basis of the *Granholm* case discussed in Case 9, and the State did not appeal. Subsequent to the district court's Commerce Clause ruling, the Washington State Legislature enacted laws extending its direct sales privilege to out-of-state wineries. The appeal to the Ninth Circuit was solely on the antitrust claims.

of the provisions of the Washington law, other than the "post-and-hold" requirements.

Section 1 of the Sherman Act provides: "Every contract, combination in the form of trust or otherwise, or conspiracy, in restraint of trade or commerce among the several States, or with foreign nations, is declared to be illegal."[4] If a group of wholesalers had met and agreed among themselves to follow the practices they were required to implement under the Washington state law, Costco would likely have had no problem proving that such actions are a violation of federal antitrust law. Should the effect be different because the state imposes the same actions on private parties legislatively, without evidence of collusion? The state argued successfully before the Ninth Circuit that anticompetitive actions, which would otherwise be prohibited under federal antitrust law, are permissible when legitimized by states under the powers granted to them by Section 2 of the Twenty-first Amendment to the Constitution. This clause, as discussed in Case 9, prohibits the transportation or importation of intoxicating liquors into any state in violation of that state's laws. The state claimed that the Sherman Act was intended to prohibit private restraints on trade, not state action. Because a state is empowered by the Twenty-first Amendment to regulate all alcohol coming into it, it can unilaterally impose pricing and related restrictions without being subjected to Sherman Act claims. The district court had agreed with the state that it, when acting as a sovereign, can impose restraints on competition because it is immune from antitrust liability.

However, Costco argued—and the district court had agreed—that the restraints in question were "hybrid": the wholesalers played an important role in implementing and enforcing

---

4. 15 U.S.C. § 1.

the state system, and in particular the post-and-hold requirement. In this respect, the state LCB allowed the producers to dic-
tate market conditions to others, and therefore the restrictions
were illegal per se under the Sherman Act. Because active state
supervision was lacking, there could be no immunity. (The lower
court did not agree with Costco's more aggressive argument that
the wholesaler industry had effectively taken over the LCB and
had written the state's legislation to perpetuate their monopoly.)

Costco also argued that keeping the current system in place
harms consumers by keeping prices high and limiting consumer
options. The state countered that keeping the current pricing
regulation system in place helped prevent alcoholism by keeping
prices higher. It actually claimed that if prices for wine in Washington fell, the state would encounter rates of alcoholism among
its residents similar to those in Russia, where alcohol was historically cheap. The Washington Beer and Wine Wholesalers Association (WBWA), which had intervened in the case as a co-defen-
dant with the LCB, made another argument: removal of the
mandatory markup would drive smaller retailers out of business
because of the increased competition. If the lower court's decision were upheld, they argued, large-volume retailers such as
Costco would be able to negotiate for price discounts and other
concessions that, as a practical matter, would not be equally
available to small-store owners. If the Ninth Circuit were to up-
hold the district court's ruling, the wholesalers maintained, the
result would be fewer choices for consumers, fewer independent
retailers in the marketplace, and fewer options for small wineries to get their product into retail shops.[5]

After considering all the parties' arguments, the Ninth Cir-

---

5. The wholesalers did not see the irony in their making these arguments—the
consolidation in the distribution industry had already had the foretold impact on consumers, small retailers, and small wineries.

cuit ruled against Costco in upholding seven of the nine challenged liquor control laws. The district court had considered the full impact of the restrictions when taken as a whole in determining their antitrust impact. The Ninth Circuit considered each on a stand-alone basis and determined that, although the post-and-hold requirement was in violation of antitrust laws, the others were a reasonable application of the state's powers under Section 2 of the Twenty-first Amendment.

This decision has initially been viewed as a victory for the alcohol distribution industry and small retailers. A decision in Costco's favor would have affected regulations in other states within the Ninth Circuit's jurisdiction and could easily have had a ripple effect on state alcoholic beverage control laws elsewhere. Costco immediately announced its intention to pursue this case, and in February 2008 it filed a petition for a rehearing by the same panel of judges. The petition also asked for an *en banc* review of the case, i.e., that the entire appeals court hear the case if the original panel did not grant Costco's request. In its brief filed in connection with the request for the rehearing, Costco stated that "Washington eliminates major aspects of ordinary competition among wine and beer producers and distributors, encouraging those private sellers to inflate prices ultimately paid by consumers."[6] On April 1, 2008, in a sort of April Fool's joke on Costco, the Ninth Circuit denied Costco's request for a rehearing and its petition for *en banc* review. The Court mandated that the Washington state LCB replace the existing post-and-hold system within seven days of the ruling. On April 8, 2008, the state LCB announced that the uniform pricing would remain in place and that all price changes had to remain in effect until changed. Pro-

---

6. Costco Wholesale Corporation's Petition for Rehearing or Rehearing en Banc, filed Feb. 18, 2008.

ducers are no longer required to hold prices in effect for a specified period of time but are still required to file all price changes on the LCB's site before they can sell, and they are required to reasonably notify all their customers when prices change. And the 10 percent markup requirement also remains in effect. On June 10, 2008, Costco announced that it would not appeal this decision to the U.S. Supreme Court.[7]

7. Washington State Liquor Control Board official website, http://www.liq.wa.gov/ 3++f-site/Costco-documents/asp.

The Taste of Wine—

Wine Appellations and the Importance of Terroir

Bronco Wine Company v. Jolly, 129 Cal. App. 4th 989 (3d Dist. 2005), *cert. denied*, ___ U.S. ___, 126 S. Ct. 1169 (2006)

When Warren Winiarski was first determining in 1970 where to locate the winery that became the famous Stag's Leap Wine Cellars, he tasted wines made from grapes in the various sub-regions of the Napa Valley and ultimately decided that the chalky soil near the cliffs of Stag's Leap produced the type of Cabernet Sauvignon grapes that he wanted for the premium Bordeaux-style blend that he intended to create.[1] Other fine wine producers in the Napa Valley and elsewhere have followed this same principle: that the nature of the soil, the climate of a geographic location, exposure to sun, water levels, slope and elevation will strongly affect the taste of the wines produced from grapes grown there. The French call this *terroir*. The wine will express a "sense of place."

---

1. Stag's Leap Wine Cellars official website, http://www.cask23.com/founders-viscon.htm

Several holiday seasons ago, a colleague from my office offered me a bottle of wine as a gift. It was a Chardonnay that I did
not know, under the label of "Charles Shaw." I was impressed
that a person I hardly knew had been so thoughtful. When I
drank it, however, I was disappointed, for the wine was, although
a decent table wine, without distinction and not of a quality that
one generally expects in a wine that one has received as a gift. I
could detect none of that "sense of place" that one finds in a
good Napa Valley Chardonnay. Very soon after, I learned that this
wine was a so-called "value wine," available only in Trader Joe's
stores, priced at $1.99 per bottle and commonly known as "Two-
Buck Chuck." (I saw this same wine several weeks later in a
Trader Joe's in Chicago, only there it was referred to as "Three-
Buck Chuck," to take into account higher distribution costs in
Illinois.) But I wondered how the Bronco Wine Company, the
producer of Charles Shaw wines, could sell what was still a relatively decent everyday table wine at such a low price. I learned
that Bronco, based in Ceres, California, produced not just the
now-famous Two-Buck Chuck but other commonly found
brands; it is the fourth-largest producer of wine in the United
States.[2] Most of its 35,000 acres of vineyards are located in California's Central Valley, far away from the Napa Valley, not just in
distance but also in terms of soil characteristics, climate, sun-
light, and availability of water. The grapes grown there are much
less expensive than Napa Valley grapes. The wines made from
them present a very different *terroir* from those produced from
Napa Valley grapes.

Others of the Bronco Wine Company's wines, however, have
been more controversial than the popular Two-Buck Chuck. As

---

2. Claim of Bronco's head, Fred Franzia, *see*, *Fred Franzia's Role in California
Wine Industry—The Story of Fred Franzia and Two Buck Chuck*, http://
www.fredfranzia.com/FredFranziaRole.aspx.

the Napa Valley developed an international reputation over the last two decades of the twentieth century for producing superior-quality wines, and as wines such as Winiarski's famous Stag's Leap Wine Cellars Cabernet Sauvignon gained critical acclaim and won awards, concerns grew over the accuracy of the place names on wine labels. It helped, of course, that the enhanced cachet of their wines enabled Napa Valley vintners to command a premium in the pricing of wines carrying a "Napa" appellation on their labels. And there was the general feeling among Napa Valley winemakers in particular that they had worked hard to lift up the general reputation of California wines from the days both before and after Prohibition, when poor-quality, generic wines had flooded the market and given all California wines a bad reputation. Accordingly, they began to clamor for increased protection for true Napa Valley wines to differentiate them from wines that had the word "Napa" in their brand names but were made from grapes grown in areas outside of the Napa Valley. They argued that wines labeled "Napa" that were not produced from Napa County grapes caused consumer confusion, especially for those novice buyers who were not familiar with specific Napa Valley wineries and were merely seeking a good-quality wine.[3] To them, "Napa" was synonymous with quality. In response to these growing concerns, in 2000 the California legislature enacted a law[4] that prevents the use of the name of a recognized viticultural region within Napa County unless a large percentage of the grapes used for the production of the wine sold under that brand came from that area.

Shortly after this legislation became effective, the California

---

3. Maura Dolan and Jerry Hirsch, *Napa Vintners Toast California's Justices*, LOS ANGELES TIMES, Aug. 6, 2004 (Business (C-1)), http://www.articles.latimes.com/2004/aug/06/business/fi-wine6.

4. CAL. BUS. & PROF. CODE § 25241.

Alcoholic Beverage Control Board (ABC) notified Bronco Wine Company that certain of its labels violated the new law. Besides Charles Shaw wines, Bronco also marketed wines made from grapes grown in areas outside the Napa Valley under the brands "Napa Ridge," "Napa Creek Winery," and "Rutherford Vintners"— areas where the cost of grapes and their perceived quality were much lower. Before 2000, Bronco had legally been entitled to sell its wines under these labels under an exception to the federal wine-labeling laws.[5]

On its Napa Creek Winery label, for example, in smaller lettering and below the brand name, Bronco stated the appellation of origin—the geographic source of the grapes—as Lodi, followed underneath by the varietal name, Chardonnay. The back label for the wine stated that the wine was "vinted and bottled" by the named winery in Napa, California. Most consumers would not know without doing some research that the word "vinted" is used when wine is fermented at one address and finished (such as by filtering out sediment) in another. Thus, in the case of the Napa Creek–labeled wine, Bronco grew and fermented the grapes in Lodi and then transported them to Bronco's bottling facility in the city of Napa, at the southern edge of the Napa Valley, for "vinting." The Napa Creek Winery back label also stated that the Chardonnay was from "vineyards blessed by the warm days and cool nights of California's *famed* [emphasis added] Lodi viticultural area," implying a region with a *terroir* as significant as the Napa Valley, when most residents of Lodi would not think of their region as "famed" among wine-producing regions.

Bronco had acquired these three brand names and the right to use the labels from predecessor wineries located in Napa County. It had acquired the Napa Ridge brand in January 2000

---

5. 27 C.F.R. § 4.39(i)(2)(ii).

from Beringer Wine Estates for more than $40 million. This brand had been in use since the early 1970s. Berenger had used the Napa Ridge brand and label for wines made from grapes grown outside the Napa Valley, including California's Central Coast and North Coast, as well as from Napa County. The owner of the Napa Creek Winery brand and the owner of the Rutherford Vintners brand had previously marketed wines under those brands made largely from Napa County grapes. After Bronco acquired these brands, they were used exclusively to sell wines made from grapes grown outside Napa County and priced generally at under $10 per bottle.

Bronco's labeling practices were legal under the relevant federal labeling regulations. Brands coming into use after 1986 when federal labeling regulations were modified were required to comply with "geographical designation requirements," including a mandate that at least 75 percent of the grapes used in the wine had to be grown in the area indicated on the label. But, as noted, brands previously in use had been "grandfathered" when the federal regulations were enacted and were allowed to be used as long as the labels also indicated the grapes' place of origin or made some statement to "dispel the impression that the geographic area suggested by the brand name is indicative of the origin of the wine."[6] All three of Bronco's labels had been in use since 1986 (although not by Bronco) and therefore, Bronco claimed, fell into this exception.

When Bronco received its notice from the California ABC, it sued, seeking a declaration that the California law was not enforceable because it was preempted by federal labeling laws. Bronco also claimed that the law violated its First Amendment Right of free speech, the Commerce Clause, and the Fifth

---

6. 27 C.F.R. § 4.39(i)(2)(iii).

Amendment Takings Clause (because the law deprived it of the value of its brand without just compensation). The lower courts found that the federal law did preempt California law,[7] but the California Supreme Court reversed, finding no preemption, and remanded the case to the California appellate court for a determination of the various other claims made by Bronco.[8] According to the California Supreme Court, states have historically taken the lead in protecting consumers against misleading brand names and labels, and there was no evidence that the federal government intended to preempt these laws when it put in place minimum standards for wine bottle labels. The court stated, "We do not find it surprising that Congress, in its effort to provide minimum standards for wine labels, would not foreclose a state with particular expertise and interest from providing stricter protection for consumers in order to ensure the integrity of its wine industry."

In its decision upon remand, the California appellate court determined that the California law preventing the use of the word "Napa" in labels on wines made from grapes not grown in Napa County was not a violation of Bronco's First Amendment rights, nor was it a violation of the Commerce Clause or the Takings Clause.

Under the First Amendment to the U.S. Constitution, commercial speech is entitled to protection from unreasonable governmental regulation, but this provides less protection than other forms of constitutionally guaranteed speech. The court noted that there has to be a balance between the commercial rights of the business to advertise its wines and the responsibility of the government to protect against claims on labels that are

---

7. Bronco Wine Co. v. Espinoza, 104 Cal. App. 4th 598 (3d Dist. 2002).
8. Bronco Wine Co. v. Jolly, 33 Cal. 4th 942 (2004).

unlawful or misleading. In this case, Bronco's brands included a geographical or viticultural designation that conveyed "information about the geographic source of the grapes used to make the wine. For that reason, a brand name of geographical significance is entitled to First Amendment protection as commercial speech only if the information about the source of the wine is accurate." Bronco claimed that consumers were not misled by the labels on its wines because they gave the geographic source of the grapes, such as Lodi.

The court disagreed and noted two things. First, a wine consumer not familiar with California geography could reasonably conclude that Lodi was located within Napa County. Second, a consumer buying wine by the glass in a restaurant would have no information about the wine other than its varietal name, such as Chardonnay, and its brand—"Napa Creek Winery"—and would assume that he or she was buying a glass of Chardonnay from the Napa Valley. Because a brand name using "Napa" is naturally associated with grapes from the Napa Valley, the consumer could easily conclude in either of the above scenarios that the wine being purchased was made from Napa Valley grapes and was of premium quality.

Polls that were presented as evidence at the trial demonstrated the accuracy of these conclusions. In a marketing survey commissioned by the California Legislature when considering the enactment of the California labeling law, 91 percent of the respondents believed that it was deceptive to use a geographic region reputed for its quality wines in a brand name if the grapes came from another region; 82 percent stated that the brand name was a critical factor in the decision to purchase a wine.

Moreover, the court suggested that Bronco itself knew that the labels would cause consumer confusion and that it took advantage of that potential confusion in the use of its labels. It noted that Bronco had spent $40 million for the Napa Ridge brand, although it did not acquire either the vineyards or the winery that had produced the Napa Ridge wine in the past. "It is reasonable to assume," the court stated, that "Bronco concluded the name 'Napa Ridge,' by itself, is valuable because it has name recognition that signifies quality." "However," the court continued, "if the wine produced under such a name is not made with Napa Valley grapes, it is marketed as something that it is not while benefiting from the reputation of Napa Valley wines."

Therefore, the court concluded that Bronco's brand names were inherently misleading and, as a result, that this commercial speech was unprotected and could be limited to prevent consumer confusion.

Bronco also claimed that the California statute violated the Commerce Clause of the U.S. Constitution because it was an attempt by the state of California to regulate products sold in interstate commerce. The court gave short shrift to this argument because the statute applied only to wine sold or offered for sale in California. Even though it might affect interstate commerce in an indirect way, its goal was not to restrict the sale of wines, but only the way wines sold in California could be labeled to prevent confusion among California consumers and to protect the reputation of the Napa Valley.

Finally, Bronco tried to convince the court that the law was an unconstitutional taking of property without just compensation because it amounted to confiscation of its federal Certificates of Label Approval (COLAs) that it had received for its three brand names. The court did not deem these COLAs to afford a property right to Bronco because they did not give Bronco any exclusive use of the brand name. Moreover, the California law did not prevent Bronco from selling its wines and, therefore, did not destroy the substantial economic value of Bronco's business.

In other words, nothing prevented Bronco from continuing to use the brands; it just had to use them on wines that complied with the statute, that is, on wines made from grapes grown in the Napa Valley.

Bronco, unhappy with this decision, took its appeals all the way to the U.S. Supreme Court in January 2006 for a second time, and for a second time the Court declined to take the case. In the aftermath, after losing numerous rounds in the courts over a four-year period, Bronco agreed to drop the word "Napa" and to add "Lodi" to its labels for wine made from grapes grown outside the Napa Valley. It agreed to change "Napa Ridge" to "Harlow Ridge," named after the street in the town of Napa where Bronco ran a large bottling plant. The label notes that the grapes are from Lodi. Bronco also agreed to use Napa grapes in its Rutherford Vintners and its Napa Creek wines. It had been more of a matter of principle for Bronco to fight so long and so hard to continue a practice that many viewed as "sneaky" but that Bronco maintained was long-standing practice in California wine making. Fred Franzia, Bronco's owner, simply did not believe that using appellations had much substance and that it was all a bit of snobbery, a symptom of the changing Napa Valley with which he disagreed.[9] Bronco's biggest cost from the lengthy battle with the state and the other Napa Valley vintners was probably the attorneys' fees it likely had to pay for the prolonged litigation, because the three brands that it defended had accounted for only a small percentage of Bronco's then $500 million in wine sales.

---

9. W. Blake Gray, *Two Buck Chuck Creator Ups the Ante in Wine Feud*, SAN FRANCISCO CHRONICLE, Thurs., May 18, 2006, http://www.sfgate.com/cgi-bin/article.cgi?f=/c/a/2006/05/18/WICGOISRON1.DTL.

Wine Labels—
Appellation of Origin

One of the most critical decisions to be made by a new winery owner is the form of, and text on, the label under which the wine will be marketed and sold. Certainly the trademark is important, and with the proliferation of so many wineries in the last few decades, coming up with a strong, eye-catching brand for a wine is increasingly difficult. But choosing the brand is only a small part of the task. A wine bottle label is used to provide the consumer with useful information to help him or her select and appreciate the wine. And frankly, it also has the purpose of selling the wine—of making the wine appear better, and of better value, than the wine next to it on the shelf.

A minimum amount of information is required by law to be on wine bottle labels in the United States. Many wineries provide additional information that they hope will influence the purchasing decision. What is on a wine label? The label, first of all, must show the brand name. If no brand is provided, then the bottler's name will be considered the brand. Many wine labels will also tell the vintage, such as 2005. This corresponds to the year of the actual grape harvest and the wine made from those grapes. If a wine is a blend of grapes from two or more years, then the wine is considered a non-vintage wine.

The label may state the "appellation of origin" for the wine and must state the wine type. It may be labeled by a grape or varietal name, such as Merlot, or it may be given a generic name, such as "Red Table Wine." Although labeling laws do not require them to do so, many wineries also list the grape varietals that comprise their generic wines. A label may also describe the wine, including any special attributes, such as whether it is sweet or dry. Many wineries will also name the vineyard where the grapes were grown, particularly if that vineyard is known for producing a high-quality grape.

The name of the producer and bottler is required by federal labeling laws, as well as their location. It is important to pay attention to the distinctions on this part of the label. "Produced and bottled by" certifies that the bottler fermented at least 75 percent of the wine. "Cellared and bottled by" indicates that the bottler aged the wine in a cellar before bottling it, but did not ferment the wine. "Bottled by" indicates that the winery bottled the wine; in other words, that the wine was grown, crushed, fermented, finished, and aged somewhere else. Opposite of "bottled by" is "estate bottled." If the label states that the wine was "estate bottled," this means that 100 percent of the grapes in the wine were grown on the winery's own vineyards, and that the winery crushed, fermented, and finished (that is, vinified) the wine, and bottled it at that winery. "Estate bottled" wine is thought to have a superior quality.

The law requires that the label show the wine's alcohol content, its net contents, and whether or not it contains sulfites. The alcohol content is shown by volume. Table wines generally have between 12 and 14 percent alcohol content. One critical step in creating the wine label is obtaining approval of the label by the federal Alcohol and Tobacco Tax Trade Bureau (TTB) within the Department of the Treasury.[1]

Under the Federal Alcohol Administration Act first enacted in 1935 and amended many times because, no person can produce, sell, or ship wine in interstate or foreign commerce without a license from the Secretary of the Treasury. For each wine so sold or shipped, the winery must obtain a Certificate of Label Approval (COLA) from the TTB that certifies that the wine label has been reviewed and approved.[2] In 1988, the FAA Act was amended further to require certain health warnings on wine labels related to consumption of alcoholic beverages during pregnancy and potential impairment of one's ability to drive a car or operate machinery.

The regulations issued under the federal act are complicated and have been amended many times. One regulation entitles a wine to be described by an appellation of origin if at least 75

Vignette (continued)

percent of the wine sold under that label comes from fruit "grown in the appellation area indicated."[3]

What is an "appellation of origin"? This term is translated from the French, *"Appellation d'Origine Contrôlée"* (AOC or AC), which is the French system for ensuring the quality of wines. This system was initiated in 1935 as a means of protecting quality vineyards and areas from unscrupulous wine producers who were making wines from other geographical areas under labels that passed the wines off as being from, and taking advantage of, better-known wine regions. The United States has modeled its structure for appellations of origin after the French system, and for the same purpose. While an appellation of origin cannot guarantee the quality of a particular winemaker's wine, it can control what goes into the making of that wine. There are seven categories in the French system that a wine must meet to quality as an AC: land, grape varieties, viticultural practices (such as the number of vines per hectare and pruning techniques), permissible yield (large yields will decrease each grape's quality), alcohol content (the grapes must reach a certain ripeness—sugar content—in order to reach a minimum alcohol level), winemaking procedures (based on historical practices that have produced favorable results), and official tasting (all wines that apply for an AC are sampled by a panel of judges).

To qualify as an appellation of origin in the United States is not so rigorous. It is a designated growing area governed by both federal and state laws and regulations.[4] This is also known as an American Viticultural Area (AVA). An appellation of origin is defined in the regulations as a political division or subdivision, a state or county, such as Napa or Sonoma County, in which grapes used to make wine are grown. A "viticultural area" is a subcategory within an appellation of origin demarcated by geographic terms and characteristics, rather than political boundaries.[5] Examples of recognized American Viticultural Areas (AVAs) include the Napa Valley and areas wholly contained within the Napa Valley, such as Rutherford, Stags Leap District, Oakville, St. Helena, and Yountville.

The other requirements for viticultural area appellation are that the area be recognized as such by the federal government, that the wine be made from at least 85 percent grapes grown in that viticultural area, and that the wine be fully finished within the state of the viticultural area. To use an appellation of origin other than an AVA on a wine label, at least 75 percent of the wine must be derived from grapes grown in the area identified by the appellation and must be fully finished in the named appellation area. To use an AVA on a wine label, the AVA must be approved under the federal regulations, 85 percent of the wine must be derived from grapes grown within the AVA, and the wine must be fully finished within the state in which the labeled AVA is located.[6]

The regulations broadly prohibit any misleading brand names. Essentially, no wine label may bear "statements, designs or devices which are false or misleading."[7]

Vignette (continued)

"No label shall contain any brand name, which, standing
alone, or in association with other printed or graphic
matter creates any impression or inference as to the age,
origin, identity, or other characteristics of the product,
unless . . . such brand name . . . conveys no erroneous
impressions as to the age, origin, identity, or other
characteristics of the product."[8]

Many times when the federal government has received a
request to designate another American Viticultural Area, there
has been a controversy between the winery or group of wineries
within that region making the request and one or more wineries
within the region that have an established brand name, but that
may not produce wine utilizing only grapes from that region. Or
the established winery may balk at having the value of its brand
weakened by the allowance of the designation for other wineries
that are less known. When the Stags Leap District was first
proposed, for example, both Stag's Leap Wine Cellars and Stags'
Leap Winery objected, because neither winery wanted to dilute
the value of its respective brand.[9] Some have complained also
that the government has moved too fast in creating these regions
without fully appreciating the nature and quality of the wines
produced there.[10]

Because of these controversies, in November 2007, in an
effort to address the effects that the approval of an AVA may
have on an established brand name, the TTB proposed revisions
to the American Viticultural Area Regulations.[11] The instigation for
this was the attempted creation of a Calistoga viticultural area in
Napa County.[12]

In its proposed rulemaking, the TTB stated its belief, based
upon comments that it had received on its initial attempt at
rulemaking to establish the Calistoga viticultural area, that a
comprehensive review of the AVA program was necessary "in
order to maintain the integrity of the program."[13] It expressed
concern that the establishment of an AVA limits the use of
established brand names, could be used by competitors to

adversely affect another winery's business, and could limit competition, because at least 85 percent of the wine using that designation must be derived from grapes grown within the AVA boundaries. It recognized that

> "establishment of a new AVA could give rise to a mislead-ing impression regarding the provenance of the wine that carries a known brand name similar to an AVA name but that does not meet the 85 percent requirement."

This could result in a failure to provide the consumer with "adequate information as to the identity and quality of the wine" and create "confusion for consumers." The TTB also noted that there had been a substantial increase in petitions to create AVAs,[14] including new AVAs within already established AVAs (so-called "nested AVAs").

The revised regulations would accordingly no longer favor place names over brand names and would impose stricter standards for the establishment of nested AVAs. And they would impose stricter requirements for the grandfathering of brands in place before the establishment of the regulations, including a double time frame: the COLA for the label with the brand must have been in place for a five-year period preceding the request for establishment of the AVA, and the label must have been in commercial use for at least three of those five years.

The comment period for the proposed regulations ended in March 2008 with many objections received. It is unlikely that the final rules will be issued before the end of 2008. But whatever decisions the government makes are likely to be controversial, especially in the emotion-laden wine production business, where appellations such as "Napa Valley" can enhance significantly both the reputation and the price of a wine, but where the creation of appellations can sometimes seem arbitrary and may also result in the dilution of an established and well-known brand. The proposed regulations make clear that, in the case of a dispute, United States regulations should generally choose to protect the established trademark over the geographic place

Vignette (continued)

name. This position puts the federal government at odds with not only those within areas such as the Napa Valley that would prefer to see greater use of geographic indications to protect the value of wine produced in those areas, but also members of the European Union.[15]

1. Created under the Homeland Security Act of 2002, formerly the Bureau of Alcohol, Tobacco and Firearms (BATF).

2. 27 C.F.R. § 4.50 (a).

3. 27 C.F.R. § 4.25(a)(1) (i)-(VI).

4. In 1978, the BATF first proposed new rules for regulating the use in brand names of terms of geographic or viticultural significance, which were amended and finally implemented in 1986.

5. 27 C.F.R. § 4.25(e)(3)(i), (ii) &-(iv).

6. 27 C.F.R. §§ 4.25 et seq.

7. 27 C.F.R. § 4.30.

8. 27 C.F.R § 4.33(b).

9. Carol Emert, *The Winiarski Way*, SAN FRANCISCO CHRONICLE, Thurs., Apr. 1, 2004, http://www.sfgate.com/cgi-bin/article.cgi?file=/c/a/2004/04/01/W1GRS5T NSF1.DTL&hw=Stags+Leap+District+Winiarski&sn=001&sc=1000.

10. Jon Bonne, *Overhaul of Labeling Rules Stirs Up Wine Wars*, SAN FRANCISCO CHRONICLE, Mon., Apr. 7, 2008, http://www.sfgate.com/cgi-bin/article.cgi?file=/c/a/2008/04/07/MN81V76JA.DTL.

11. Notice No. 78, 72 Fed. Reg. No. 223, at 65,261-75 (Nov. 20, 2007).

12. Notice No. 77, 72 Fed. Reg. No. 223, at 65,256-61 (Nov. 20, 2007).

13. *Id.*

14. There are almost 200 U.S. appellations, and within California there are more than 100.

15. *See* Case 12.

What's Bud® Got to Do with It?
Appellations and Trademarks in a Global Economy

World Trade Organization (WTO) Ruling,
WT/DS 174 R 15, March 2005 (05-0955),
(U.S. Complaint) and WT/DS 290 R 15, March 2005
(Australian Complaint) (The "Budweiser® Ruling")

Wine enthusiasts grow poetic in describing the great pleasure derived from tasting the smooth mineral flavors of a dry white wine known as "Chablis," produced in the area north of the Burgundy region of France with grapes from vines grown in the limestone soil of the region, and in inhaling the soft, earthy bouquet of an impeccably finished red wine from the Saint Emilion region northeast of Bordeaux, and in feeling against their palates the delicate bubbles of a fine sparkling wine produced in Epernay, in the heart of the Champagne region of France. These wines are all what they are because of where the grapes from which they are produced are grown, and their names, whether Chablis, Bordeaux or Champagne, tell us what to expect from the wine. Unfortunately and ironically, because of

A Champagne Vineyard

the quality of these wines, vintners from other parts of the world have "borrowed" their names to pass off very different and frequently inferior wines as something of a greater quality. This complaint has been leveled against California wines since the early days of the California wine industry in the nineteenth century. For example, winemakers in the state as early as the 1860s and 1870s gave blended red wines with no relation at all to the red wines made from Pinot Noir grapes in France's Burgundy region names such as "California Burgundy," or simply "Burgundy" wine.

The naming of wines first became common in eighteenth century France when wine was identified by the area in which the grapes were grown. Grapes grown in the Bordeaux region produced "*un vin de Bordeaux*"—that is, a wine from Bordeaux; grapes grown in the Chablis region produced "*un vin de Chablis*," and so forth. Before this time, wines were largely identified by their color. Red Burgundy wines made from the Pinot Noir grape were "*vins rouges*." Wines from the south were "*vins rosés*" —that is, with a "blush"—and wines from Bordeaux were called "clarets," from their clear, luminous, light red color. By the time winemaking activities started in California in the mid-nineteenth century, French wines had acquired an international cachet. These wines graced the dinner tables of upper-class East Coast Americans. Winemakers in California therefore followed a natural impulse to identify their wines with those from France if they might have remotely similar characteristics. For example, a French wine producer in California might have called the white California wine he had produced a "Chablis" because it had perhaps some distant characteristics of a French Chablis. This wine was not a true Chablis, however, and over time the term "Chablis" came to generically represent any light dry or semi-dry white wine, even though its only resemblance to the classic mineral-tasting dry white wine produced in the Chablis region of France was the name.

This practice has continued into the twenty-first century and remains legal within the United States. Winemakers can use what are known as "semi-generic" place names such as "Chablis" or "Chianti" or "Burgundy" on their labels as long as they also disclose the geographic region in which they are produced, such as "California Burgundy." This is the case even though there is less and less reason to give "faux" place names to California wines. When Jack and Jamie Davies founded the Schramsberg Vineyards in 1965, they called their sparkling wine "Champagne" to demonstrate to consumers that they were serious about producing a quality sparkling wine, using the "*méthode champenoise.*"[1] Another sparkling wine specialist in California, Korbel

---

1. Linda Murphy, *Napa Valley's Grande Dame: Schramsberg's Jamie Davies Coaxes Champagne Quality from California Grapes*, SAN FRANCISCO CHRONICLE, Thurs., Dec.22, 2005, http://www.sfgate.com/cgi-bin/article.cgi?file=/c/a/2005/12/22/WIGDGG 919B1.DTL&hw=Schramsberg+California+champagne&sn=001&sc=1000.

In 1973, Moët-Hennessy (Moët et Chandon) acquired land near Yountville and founded Domaine Chandon; its first California sparkling wine using the méthode champenoise was released in 1976, and its visitors' center and famed restaurant opened in 1977.

Champagne Cellars, claims to have produced sparkling wines in California since 1882 and has always identified these as "Champagne," or more recently, "California Champagne." They argue that the *"méthode champenoise"* is a method for making sparkling wine that originated in the Champagne region of France and that Champagne is not a *"terroir."* They maintain that what makes the sparkling wine great is not the quality of the grapes but the meticulous methodology used to produce the secondary fermentation that creates the sparkling wine.[2] Therefore, any consumer who appreciates good sparkling wine knows that Korbel California Champagne originates in the United States and that it is not to be confused with sparkling wines produced in and named after the famous region east of Paris. Schramsberg has taken a different tack. Since the mid-1990s, when a number of French Champagne houses such as Moët et Chandon and G. H. Mumm established wineries in Northern California—Domaine Chandon and Mumm Napa—Schramsberg has identified its famous sparkling wines simply as "Schramsberg,"

---

2. Gerald D. Boyd, *Inaccurate Labeling of "Champagne" is Making a Case of Sour Grapes*, SAN FRANCISCO CHRONICLE, Wed., Dec. 20, 2000, http://www.sfgate.com/cgibin/article.cgi?file=/c/a/2000/12/20/FD50619.DTL&hw=Korbel+California+Champagne&sn=005&sc=548.

knowing that the brand is sufficient to denote the quality of the beverage.[3]

The French have taken a strong position, attempting through regulatory means to repatriate names considered to be generic in the United States, such as Chablis and Champagne, and suggesting that wines produced in California that are identified using French place names do not possess the character or quality of a good French wine and are merely poor-quality imitators. And in all honesty, this misuse of place names in the past stigmatized California wines as being inferior to their French namesakes. As California winemakers have moved away from this particular practice toward that of placing the varietal name on the label, such as Chardonnay or Pinot Noir instead of Chablis or Burgundy, this stigma has faded.

Wines and beers that have generic names taken from registered European geographic indications (GIs),[4] although legal in the United States, are prohibited not just in France but throughout the European Union. The EU finds terms such as "California Champagne" to be deceptive and confusing to consumers as well as harmful to the image and value of wines produced in regions that rightfully claim the name of that particular place. And this conflict between the EU's efforts to protect its geographic names led the United States and Australia to lodge complaints before the World Trade Organization (WTO). The WTO's ruling in the United States' favor established and confirmed the rights of parties who had had established trademarks that were also place

---

3. Linda Murphy, *Napa Valley's Grande Dame: Schramsberg's Jamie Davies Coaxes Champagne Quality from California Grapes*, SAN FRANCISCO CHRONICLE, Thurs., Dec. 22, 2005, http://www.sfgate.com/cgi-bin/article.cgi?file=/c/a/2005/12/22/WIGDGG 919B1.DTL&hw=Schramsberg+California+champagne&sn=001&sc=1000.

4. Geographic Indications are place names—and in some countries also words associated with a place—used to identify the origin and quality, reputation or other characteristics of products such as "Champagne."

> *Fraud and adulteration were growing problems in the 19th Century, and sloppy practices in the California wine industry prevented California from developing the reputation necessary to replace the French wineries as having the best wines.*

names versus the rights of European Union members seeking to restrict the sale of beverages within their territory of products, whether wine or beer, that carry the place name of geographic significance that has been registered as such with the EU.

In 1994, the United States and member nations of the European Union, among others, signed the WTO agreement on Trade-Related Aspects of Intellectual Property Rights (TRIPS Agreement), which came into force in 1996.[5] The TRIPS Agreement requires that WTO members provide the legal means for interested parties to prevent the use of a GI that indicates or suggests that a product originates in a geographical area other than its true place of origin, in a manner that misleads the public as to the real geographic origin of the product, or that constitutes an act of unfair competition. The TRIPS Agreement also provides for an "enhanced" minimum level of protection for GIs that identify wines and spirits.[6] For wines and spirits, even if the public would not be deceived by the use of a particular GI, a GI may not be used if the wines or spirits do not originate in the place indicated by the GI. However, there are exceptions to the TRIPS Agreement. For example, TRIPS does not require protection of a GI if it is the generic or semi-generic name for the wine, such as

---

5. For developed countries.
6. TRIPS, Art. 23.

Chablis or Champagne, in the country where it is made, such as the United States. Also, if a trademark using a place name that is a GI already existed when the GI was registered, then the trademark is legally presumed to take precedence over the GI.

Before TRIPS was ratified by WTO member nations, in July 1992, the European Union had issued a regulation[7] that protected GIs and designation of origin for agricultural products and foodstuffs (including wine) within the EU. In this regulation, the European Council created a system that protected certain names by allowing for their registration. Once registered, those designations of origin and geographic indications were reserved solely for the products that had been produced and/or processed in the regions or places designated by those names. In other words, only sparkling wines produced in the Champagne region of France could be sold in the EU under the name "Champagne." Moreover, regional trade names such as "Champagne" are related to products connected to a particular territory and, unlike trademarks, do not ensure an exclusive right but are available to any producer in the region. This regulation conflicted with the practice of wineries in other parts of the world, not just in the United States, which had long used such place names to identify their wines or other beverages and viewed these names as generic.

The United States was concerned that this EU regulation provided stronger protection for GIs of EU members but denied the same level of protection to United States's GIs. This meant, for the wine industry, that places like Napa in California, or the Willamette Valley in Oregon, or Finger Lakes in New York could not be assured under the EU regulation that their names would be protected in Europe. This was because the EU regulation re-

---

7. European Council Reg. No. 2081/92 (1992).

In 1965, Jack and Jamie Davies purchased the Schramsberg Estate and began producing quality sparkling wine, using the méthode champenoise, the traditional method for making Champagne, developed in the Champagne region of northern France.

quired reciprocity; it required that non-EU countries also protect EU products, such as Chianti, Chablis, and Champagne. Because the United States and some other countries have not amended their laws to provide such protection, U.S. products such as Florida oranges or Idaho potatoes did not qualify for registration within the EU. The United States asked the WTO to force the EU to open the protections offered to EU products to other non-EU countries without requiring reciprocity.

The United States also believed that the EU regulation did not provide sufficient protection to preexisting trademarks that are similar or identical to a European GI. It claimed that the European Council regulation, as enforced by the EU, violated the TRIPS agreement because it did not ensure that an owner of a trademark registered before 1996 could prevent uses of a geographic indication that would create confusion with the established trademark. The United States claimed that the EU protections of GIs were inconsistent with its obligations under the TRIPS Agreement. The TRIPS Agreement specified that a trademark that has been used or registered in good faith in one country could not be preempted by a later-established GI that conflicted with that trademark. The EU defended its right to protect GIs and to prevent registration of trademarks within the EU that use GIs unless there was reciprocity in banning the use of EU GIs in the home country.

In 2004, the United States initiated a dispute settlement case at the WTO against the European Union. (Australia launched a comparable case at the same time.)

The United States challenged the EU regulation on several grounds. First, it claimed that the regulation allowed no national treatment for foreigners. It argued that government intervention should not be required for an owner to assert a trademark or a GI right. The EU regulation had allowed European Community right holders to apply directly to register and protect their GIs for EU-originated products, but non-European nationals had to rely on their government to apply for protection in the European Community on their behalf and to object to GI applications in the European Community. Also it disputed the EU requirement that, to obtain protection for its GIs, such as Idaho potatoes, a foreign government such as the United States had to adopt a system of protection for EU GIs that mirrored the European Community's regulation. The WTO panel agreed with the United States that these aspects of the regulation discriminated in favor of European Community products and of EU GI right holders against GI right holders and the products of non-EU WTO agreement signatories. The panel found that the conditions imposed by the EU on a non-EU member to obtain GI protection under the EU regulations violated the national treatment obligation under TRIPS, by affording less favorable treatment to non-European Community nationals than to EC nationals. For example, it protects a name such as "Champagne," but fails to protect U.S. products, such as Florida orange juice or Idaho potatoes, that are named for their place of origin.

Second, the United States argued that the European Community's GI regulation would not allow certain trademark owners to enforce their trademark rights and prevent holders of similar or identical GIs from confusing uses. The United States maintained that the TRIPS Agreement requires that the owner of a registered trademark be enabled by law to prevent others from using the same trademark that includes a GI when consumers would be confused by the later uses. The WTO panel agreed generally with the United States's interpretation of TRIPS. The panel also found that the EU Regulation was inconsistent with TRIPS because it limited the availability of use rights for owners of trademarks. In other words, the EU cannot deny U.S. trademark holders, such as Anheuser-Busch, the right to register and use its mark, such as Budweiser®, in the EU. However, the panel allowed for the coexistence of a GI in the European Union with a similar or preexisting product trademark. Nevertheless, it also ruled that the EU's GI regulations could protect only GI names as registered in their original language, but this protection could not extend to translations of the GI unless this also had been specifically registered.

And this leads to why the WTO decision is often referred to as the "Budweiser® Ruling." Why discuss a beer case in a book about wine? Because the United States's complaint to the World Trade Organization was instigated in part because of adverse actions against the Budweiser® brand in the European Union, although it had a larger purpose of clarifying and enforcing rights that broadly affected not just beer but any wine or other beverage trademarks. Anheuser-Busch had been selling beer in the United States since 1876 using the Budweiser® mark. The name was no longer associated with any particular place. Budweiser®-branded beer has been exported to a number of countries since early in the twentieth century. It is a well-known international brand. Anheuser-Busch also sells beer internationally under the BUD® brand. Budejovicky Budvar, NP, a Czech brewer, had been selling a beer called "Budweiser," named after Budvar, the place name, since 1895. The Czech Republic claimed the terms "Bud-weiser" and "BUD" were proprietary GIs that identify beer from the town of Ceske Budejovice (which translates into German as "Budweis"). This GI was registered for European Union protection in 2004. The Czech Republic also claimed protection of the name "Budweiser Bürgerbrau" as an appellation of origin for beer produced in that town under the Lisbon Agreement for the Protection of Appellations of Origin and their International Registration (Lisbon Agreement).[8] (The United States is not a signatory of the Lisbon Agreement.[9]) Under the theory that GIs are superior to trademark rights in the European Union, the brewery, Budejovicky Budvar, sought to prohibit Anheuser-Busch from selling beer under the Budweiser® name anywhere in the European Union and to cancel Anheuser-Busch's trademark registrations in several countries, including Austria, France, Germany, and Greece.

The WTO Ruling halted the attempts by Budejovicky Budvar to prevent sales of beer under the Budweiser® name in the European Union by relying on the GI registration, even though the Czech GI is still protected as registered. This conflict between the EU's regulations concerning geographic naming rights and the United States's attempt to protect Anheuser-Busch's (and other companies') right to use the same place names in long-established brand names illustrates the priorities of each country. The EU seeks to protect geographic names used to identify wine and beer for the exclusive use within those geographic areas

8. Registration No. 837, Lisbon Agreement for the Protection of Appellations of Origin and their International Registration of October 31, 1958, as revised at Stockholm on July 14, 1967, and as amended on September 28, 1979 (Lisbon Agreement).

9. Current members of the Lisbon Agreement (as of January 15, 2008) are Algeria, Bulgaria, Burkina Faso, Congo, Costa Rica, Cuba, the Czech Republic, the Democratic People's Republic of Korea, France, Gabon, Georgia, Haiti, Hungary, Iran, Israel, Italy, Mexico, Portugal, Moldova, Montenegro, Nicaragua, Peru, Portugal, Serbia, Slovakia, Togo, and Tunisia.

where specific wines and spirits are made. Therefore, for the EU it is as important to retain the name "Champagne" for all sparkling wines made from grapes from the Champagne region as it would be to protect the brands under which that wine is bottled, whether Moët et Chandon, Veuve Cliquot, or Mumm. On the other hand, in the United States, trademark protection of an established brand would have highest priority.

Even though the WTO ruling did not specifically relate to the wine sector, it nevertheless was helpful to the United States' wine industry. As noted, from the European perspective, geographical protections best trademark rights. Europe's goal is to reclaim names that relate to specific places, whether Champagne, Parmesan cheese, or Budweiser beer. But for United States producers, where these names have become generic, being forced to change them to something else would mean expensive repackaging and rebranding. The WTO ruling did not end the controversy for either beer producers or wine producers. For instance, even though everyone agreed in the TRIPS accord that wine names deserve special treatment, U.S. regulations allow some European GIs, such as Champagne, Burgundy, and Chablis, to be used by wine producers to designate products made from grapes grown in the United States, not in Champagne or Burgundy. In fact, generic wine names are provided for in wine-labeling regulations.

As the global wine industry has grown, new controversies will arise, and in fact already have surfaced. A recent EU decision illustrates the dilemma even for EU members. As more Eastern Bloc countries have joined the European Union, the Western members have faced a dilemma comparable to that faced in the United States because of long-time use of certain names. As part of the agreements for Hungary's accession to the European Union, the governments of Italy and France agreed to require that wines called "Tokay d'Alsace" (France) and "Tocai Friulano" (Italy) be renamed because the Hungarian government claimed that these names were too similar to the famous Hungarian sweet wine, Tokaji Aszu—commonly known internationally as Tokay—produced in the Tokaji region of Hungary (a GI). The Alsatians agreed to rename their wine as "Tokay-Pinot Gris d'Alsace," but the Friulians objected. "Tocai" is the name of the specific grape used in their wine. However, the EU rejected the appeal because the name of the Italian Tocai did not qualify as a geographic indication; it did not have characteristics that are attributable to its geographic region. This presented an interesting problem and also demonstrates the confusion and unfairness that can result when geographic names are supported over an existing and long-standing trademark. The Italian use of "Tocai" did not reflect the same situation as California winemakers calling a generic blended red wine a "Burgundy," because for the Hungarians, Alsatians, and Italians in the case of Tocai, the three wines in question were all very different. The French and Italians were not attempting to take advantage of the reputation of the Hungarian wine by imitating its style, or by attempting to pass off inferior wine as something better. The Tokay d'Alsace was a light, dry wine made entirely from the Pinot Gris grape. The Italian Tocai Friulano was a dry white wine also, but more aromatic, made from the Tocai grape (Sauvignon Vert). The Hungarian Tokaji Aszu is a dessert wine made from other (not Tocai) grapes that have been afflicted with botrytis (noble rot). The Italians particularly were very disappointed with the EU decision because they could not see why the makers of a wine named after a place in Hungary (Tokaji) but not made from Tocai grapes could claim priority over or have superior rights to those held by the Italian makers of Tocai Friulano, which is made entirely from the Tocai grape.

And for California winemakers, turnabout may seem ultimately to be fair play. Napa Valley winemakers have come to appreciate better in the last few years the Europeans' position on the importance of *terroir* and place names. At the same time the United States was challenging the European Union regulation at the WTO and arguing in favor of the priority of long-standing trademarks over GIs, its own labeling laws were under scrutiny in the legal battle pitting Napa Valley winemakers and the state of California against the Bronco Wine Company, to prohibit Bronco from "borrowing" the Napa Valley name in its trademarks to sell wines from grapes not grown in the Napa Valley.[10] In 2007, the Napa Valley became the first U.S. wine region to win recognition from the European Union as a Geographic Indication, entitling its wines to recognition and protection by the EU's member nations. A big victory for wines that were disparaged just a century before.

Indeed, the legal and wine worlds are full of ironies.

---

10. *See* Case 11.

What are "Geographic Indications"?

"Geographic indications" are commonly referred to as signs to indicate the regional origin of a particular good, such as wine or beer. They can convey to consumers some of the important or desirable characteristics of the goods or services that are attributable to their geographic origin. They are valued for the same reason that trademarks are valued: they identify the source of the product. They point out that the product, instead of coming from a particular manufacturer, has been produced in a certain territory or region. They also are an indicator of quality: the consumer knows that the product comes from a region recognized for a superior product. They also are intended to protect products and producers in a particular region from unfair competition.

Geographic indications have become so important today because, like trademarks, they are valuable marketing tools in a global economy. And in the case of certain geographic areas, such as Champagne, for example, there is a strong desire to take back a term that has long been generically used in some countries, through enforcement of geographic indications regulations.

The conflict between those desires and the concerns of owners of long-established trademarks that use place names came out in the open in the negotiations for the International Agreement on Trade-Related Aspects of Intellectual Property Rights (TRIPS) in the December 1993 Uruguay Round of the General Agreement on Tariffs and Trade (GATT). Each signatory to the TRIPS accord, which included the United States and the then member nations of the European Union, agreed to abide by the treaty and to recognize the intellectual property rights (including trademark rights) of owners within each of the signatory countries.

The TRIPS Agreement sets forth standards to regulate international intellectual property protection and enforcement

Vignette (continued)

and establishes international minimum standards for geographic indications. For purposes of TRIPS, geographic indications are defined as follows:

"[I]ndications which identify a good as originating in the territory of a member, or a region or locality in that territory, where a given quality, reputation, or other characteristic of the good is essentially attributable to its geographic origin."[1]

Examples of geographic indications in the United States are Florida for oranges, Idaho for potatoes, Washington state for apples, and Vidalia for onions. Under Article 22, all governments must provide legal opportunities in their own laws for the owner of a geographic indication registered in that country to prevent the use of misleading trademarks.

Article 23 of TRIPS provides an enhanced level of protection for geographic indications for wines and beers. Under Article 23, all governments must provide the owners of geographic indications the right, under their laws, to prevent the use of a geographical indication identifying wines not originating in the place indicated by such geographical indication. It absolutely prohibits the registration of any trademark containing a false geographic indication as a source of wines and beers, regardless of whether the public would actually be deceived or whether the location is obscure or remote. These provisions took effect on January 1, 1996.

Although geographic indications are protected in theory under the TRIPS Agreement, as a practical matter the agreement sets out only minimum standards of protection, with certain exceptions. In the absence of international consensus among World Trade Organization members, including the United States and the member counties of the European Union, various participants in the negotiations for the agreement were divided over the protection that must be afforded to intellectual property rights in geographic indications under TRIPS.[2] The United States was concerned that trademark protection for long-standing and established brands could be obliterated by this new agreement. Accordingly, it fought hard for certain protective exceptions. For example, under TRIPS, names that have become common or generic (such as Cheddar cheese in the United States) can be used whether or not they use a false geographic indication. Thus, despite TRIPS, because "Champagne" is recognized in the United States as a semi-generic term,[3] it can continue to be used for any "light-colored sparkling wine with bubbles." Accordingly, Korbel Champagne Cellars, for example, can continue to legally identify its sparkling wine as "California Champagne" because it had used the name in connection with its sparkling wines long before 1996.

In addition, restrictions do not apply to the continued registration of geographic indications—however false or misleading—that were first used in established trademarks. Where a trademark had been applied for or registered in good faith, or where rights to a trademark have been acquired through actual use in good faith, either before January 1, 1996, or before the geographical indication was protected in its country of origin, the trademark maintains its legal presumption of superiority, based on the principle of "first-in-time, first-in-right." When the federal trademark law (Lanham Act) was amended to implement TRIPS,[4] these exceptions for prior trademark use were specifically carved out.[5] The amendment prohibits registration of "a geographic indication which, when used on or in connection with wines or spirits, identifies a place other than the origin of the goods" and is first used in connection with wines, for example, by the applicant on or after January 1, 1996.

---

1. International Agreement on Trade-Related Aspects of Intellectual Property Rights (TRIPS), Article 22(1).

2. *See, e.g.,* the Communications from Canada, Chile, Japan, and the United States, IP/C/W/133/Rev. www.wto.org.

3. *See* federal wine-labeling regulations, 27 C.F.R. § 4.24(b)(2). According to the regulation, semi-generic designations may be used to designate wines of an origin other than that indicated by such name only if there appears in direct conjunction therewith an appropriate appellation of origin disclosing the true place of origin of the wine, such as "California Champagne." 27 C.F.R. § 4.24(a)(1).

4. 15 U.S.C. § 1052(a).

5. 15 U.S.C. § 1052(f).

About the Author

Carol Robertson has been a practicing attorney for over 25 years, including as a partner at a major San Francisco law firm and as corporate counsel with San Francisco Bay Area companies. In the course of her practice, Ms. Robertson has had the opportunity to represent grape growers, wine producers, and alcoholic beverage retailers in their general business and regulatory matters. She

Carol Robertson

has taught French at both the high school and college levels, and holds a BA and an MA in French Literature. She interrupted her studies toward her PhD in order to attend law school at the University of California at Berkeley (Boalt Hall School of Law), where she graduated in the top 10 percent of her class in 1980.

She has been a frequent speaker at professional seminars, workshops, conferences and conventions throughout the United States and Canada, on various business and legal subjects, and has taught English at the Law and Business School and at the College of Sciences at the Université de Pau, France. Ms. Robertson is an adjunct professor at John F. Kennedy University, in Pleasant Hill, California, in the School of Management and in the Law School, where she has taught courses on Business Law, Business Ethics, and Negotiation Techniques.

Ms. Robertson has been a wine enthusiast since her college years when she studied at the Université de Bordeaux, in France, where she earned a Diplôme Supérieur d'Etudes Françaises. During one of her frequent trips back to France, she was inducted as an honorary member of the Compagnons du Bordeaux, a local wine guild, whose mission is to foster the reputation of Bordeaux wines.